READING COMPREHENSION SERIES • LEVEL BB

MANES AND REINS

Martha K. Resnick
Carolyn J. Hyatt

STECK-VAUGHN
COMPANY
A Subsidiary of National Education Corporation

About the Authors

MARTHA K. RESNICK is an experienced elementary teacher, formerly a Reading Resource Teacher with the Baltimore City Schools. She has served as a cooperative practice teacher, training student teachers from many colleges. Mrs. Resnick received her master's degree in education at Loyola College.

CAROLYN J. HYATT has taught elementary, secondary, and adult education classes. She was formerly a Senior Teacher with the Baltimore City Schools. Mrs. Hyatt received her master's degree in education at Loyola College.

Reading Comprehension Series

Wags & Tags

Claws & Paws

Gills & Bills

Manes & Reins

Bones & Stones

Swells & Shells

Heights & Flights

Trails & Dales

Acknowledgments

Illustrated by Rosemarie Fox-Hicks, Sue Durban, and David Cunningham

Cover design Linda Adkins Design

Cover photograph © Ron Kimball Photography

All photographs used with permission. Interior photographs: © 1988 Graphic Masters Inc./David Roth; © 1988 Kenji Kerins

ISBN 0-8114-1345-4

2 3 4 5 6 7 8 9 PO 95 94 93

Contents

Story 1..4
A Vocabulary   **B** Facts & Inferences   **C** Noting Details/ Picture Comprehension   **D** Classifying   **E** Main Idea of Paragraphs   **F** Noting Details/Sentence Comprehension

Story 2..10
A Facts & Inferences
B Noting Details/Understanding Time Relationships
C Predicting Outcomes   **D** Vocabulary

Story 3..16
A Facts & Inferences   **B** Multiple Meanings
C Drawing Conclusions   **D** Using Context Clues
E Main Idea of Paragraphs   **F** Vocabulary

Story 4..22
A Facts & Inferences   **B** Noting Details
C Vocabulary in Context   **D** Using Context Clues
E Sequencing

Story 5..28
A Facts & Inferences   **B** & **C** Understanding Paragraph Structure   **D** Main Idea   **E** Picture/Story Comprehension   **F** Extraneous Sentences in Paragraph   **G** Vocabulary   **H** Predicting Outcomes
I Noting Details/Picture Comprehension

Skills Review (Stories 1–5)......34
A Understanding Paragraph Structure   **B** Writing a Paragraph   **C** Picture/Story Comprehension
D Following Directions   **E** Multiple Meanings
F Using Context Clues   **G** Vocabulary in Context
H Main Idea of Paragraphs   **I** Vocabulary

Story 6..40
A Facts & Inferences   **B** & **C** Understanding Paragraph Structure   **D** Vocabulary in Context
E Multiple Meanings   **F** Writing a Paragraph
G Punctuation   **H** Drawing Conclusions

Story 7..46
A Facts & Inferences   **B** Understanding Time Relationships   **C** Understanding the Calendar
D Sequencing   **E** Understanding the Calendar
F Vocabulary   **G** Drawing Conclusions

Story 8..52
A Facts & Inferences   **B** & **C** Sequencing
D Vocabulary   **E** Noting Details
F & **G** Sequencing

Story 9..58
A Facts & Inferences   **B** & **C** Sequencing
D Noting Details/Writing Sentences   **E** Vocabulary
F Vocabulary in Context   **G** Sequencing

Story 10..64
A Facts & Inferences **B** Vocabulary
C & **D** Understanding Time Relationships: Seasons
E & **F** Understanding Time Relationships: Months
G Sequencing

Skills Review (Stories 6–10)....70
A Sequencing   **B** Vocabulary in Context
C & **D** Sequencing   **E** Drawing Conclusions
F Antonyms   **G** Drawing Conclusions

Story 11..76
A Facts & Inferences   **B** Understanding Conversation   **C** Vocabulary
D & **E** Understanding Quotation Marks
F Understanding Conversation in Cartoons

Story 12..82
A Facts & Inferences   **B** Using a Table of Contents
C Vocabulary   **D** Using a Table of Contents: Classifying   **E** Making a Table of Contents
F Comprehending Absurdities

Story 13..88
A Facts & Inferences   **B** Vocabulary   **C** Following Directions   **D** Making Judgments   **E** Predicting Outcomes

Story 14..94
A Making Inferences   **B** & **C** Making Inferences from Cartoons   **D** Vocabulary   **E** Making Inferences Using Mathematics

Story 15..100
A Facts & Inferences   **B** Using a Picture Dictionary
C Understanding Conversation in Cartoons
D Vocabulary

Skills Review (Stories 11–15) 106
A & **B** Using a Table of Contents   **C** Using Context Clues   **D** Vocabulary in Context   **E** Predicting Outcomes   **F** Making Judgments   **G** Making Inferences Using Mathematics   **H** Understanding Quotation Marks   **I** Making Inferences

Do any of the police officers in your city ride horses? Some cities do have mounted police. One of these cities is Baltimore, Maryland.

A soldier started the horse police in Baltimore many years ago. Now there are more of them because horses can get out of traffic jams better than police cars.

For many years the most popular police horse was a big brown horse with a black mane named Mike. When Mike went to work for the city, he was a little wild. Mike stood up on his hind legs and the rider slid off. Police Officer Bob was the only one strong enough to stay on Mike's back. Even he was sometimes thrown off and landed in the street.

After sliding off Mike several times, Bob got tired of landing on his back in the street with everyone laughing. So Bob learned to hold on tightly to the reins with both hands. That way he could control tricky Mike better.

After a time the big horse became as gentle as a lamb. Bob, on top of Mike, directed traffic, rode in parades, and posed for thousands of pictures people took. Children often came up to feed apples or carrots to the horse they loved.

On streets where houses came up to the sidewalk, Bob often rode Mike right up to the windows to see sick people. The people could come to the window and pat Mike on his nose. It made them happy to have the horse visit.

But Bob and Mike had hard jobs, too. They galloped down back streets and cut off racing bank robbers. If there were fights, the police officer and horse could break them up.

Mike had good care. He lived in a nice stall. He had people to wash him, brush his mane, and feed him. A vet came when he was sick. A blacksmith put new horseshoes on Mike whenever he needed them.

Now Mike is too old to work. Bob has found him a home on a farm. Of course, Bob comes to visit his four-legged friend often.

A **Read the words in the Word Box. Write the correct words next to the meanings.**

Word Box	popular	reins	hind
	wild	mane	gallop
	mounted	gentle	stall

1. liked by many people   _____

2. place where a horse sleeps   _____

3. back legs   _____

4. opposite of wild   _____

5. got up on a horse   _____

6. hair on a horse's neck   _____

7. ride very quickly   _____

8. hard to control   _____

1. What is this story mainly about?

   a. how people train wild horses

   b. how a vet and a blacksmith take care of horses

   c. how a man and an animal worked together

2. When did the wild horse become as gentle as a lamb?

   a. before Bob fell in the street

   b. after Bob could control him

   c. before people laughed at Bob

3. How do horses help the police?

   a. They carry food for them.

   b. They help the police keep traffic moving.

   c. They bring doctors to sick people.

4. What is another job Bob and Mike did?

   a. They rode in parades.

   b. They ran after runaway cows.

   c. They took money to banks.

5. How do we know the horse was popular with children?

   a. Someone made up a song about him.

   b. Children got new reins for the horse.

   c. Children took food to him.

6. Who takes care of sick horses?

   a. a vet

   b. a blacksmith

   c. people who are ill

7. How did Bob teach Mike not to be wild?

   a. He told him to be gentle.

   b. He controlled him with the reins.

   c. He took him to the vet.

6

C Draw a line from each sentence to the right picture.
One is done for you.

a.

b.

1. Hand the toy to me.
2. Put your hand on the chair.

c.

d.

3. He leaves the stall.
4. The leaves are green.

e.

f.
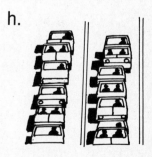

5. The rock is large.
6. See the chair rock.

g.
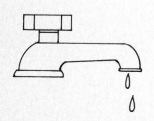

h.

7. It is hard to move in a
   traffic jam.
8. Put some jam on the bread.

i.

j.

9. She drops the book.
10. Drops of water came out.

Here is Mike. Label each part on the animal.
Use one word from each pair of words.

Labels		
mane, man	run, reins	not, nose
mount, mouth	tail, tall	legs, leaves
saddle, stall	ears, hears	

1. _____

2. _____

3. _____

4. _____

5. _____

6. _____

7. _____

8. _____

E Read the stories. Pick the right title that tells the main idea of each story from the box. Write it on the line over the story.

Titles
a. Who Started the Mounted Police
b. How the Mounted Police Are Trained
c. What Mounted Police Wear

1. _____

The mounted police officers wore dark blue riding pants with black boots. Their helmets were white and gold. Their jackets were dark blue and yellow.

2. _____

Police officers who are picked to work with horses must be trained. First, they learn to feed and brush their horses. Then they learn to take care of everything the horse must have on. The officers also learn how to ride in traffic and on city streets.

F **<u>Underline</u> the sentence which best tells about each picture.**

1.

   a. Bob holds the reins.

   b. Bob dropped the reins.

   c. The reins are on the horse's feet.

2.

   a. The horse stands still.

   b. The horse is in his stall.

   c. The horse is galloping.

3.

   a. The animal controls the person.

   b. The woman controls the traffic.

   c. The woman controls the animal.

4.

   a. The horse's mane is not long.

   b. The mane is on the animal's neck.

   c. The man is doing his job.

5.

   a. She mounted the horse.

   b. She was gentle with her pets.

   c. She was galloping wildly.

Anita was eight years old. Her little brother Gilbert was only three, but he wanted to do everything Anita did. He wanted to go everywhere she went.

Anita had her own secret place. It was a tiny room on the third floor of her house. It was the only place Anita could go to get away from Gilbert. She often heard Gilbert calling her when she was in her room. But he could never find her.

On a warm Thursday in April, Anita opened the window of her room. She forgot to shut it when she left. The next day, she found two birds building a neat little nest on the window sill.

Anita stood very still. She did not make a sound. The birds looked at her, and she looked at them. Soon the birds trusted Anita, so they kept on with their building.

Day after day, Anita saw these wonderful sights.

Three Weeks Later

The three baby birds chirped and called. Their bills were always open. Their parents had to work hard to feed them. Anita was always quiet and still so she would not frighten the hard-working parents or their babies.

"The big birds need help," thought Anita. She got these things for her feathered friends.

Just as the sun was coming up, Anita was in the kitchen. She put all these things into a small bowl with some water. She mashed them with a fork. Now she had some soft food for the birds.

Later that day, Anita put a tiny bit of mashed food into each chirping baby bird's mouth. They loved it! They cried for more!

Every day after that Anita fed the baby birds. One day when she was in her secret room, Gilbert found her. He followed her in. "Quiet, Shhh!" Anita whispered.

They tiptoed out of the room. Gilbert didn't want to leave. He wanted to feed the baby birds, too.

"No, you're too little," said Anita.

Gilbert started to cry. Anita didn't want their parents to find out she was feeding the birds. She had to give in to Gilbert.

Gilbert was as quiet as a mouse. He watched his sister put a tiny bit of food into one baby bird's mouth. Then Anita put some food on Gilbert's little finger. She held him while he fed some mashed food to one of the birds.

The baby bird was hungry. It ate all the food. Gilbert was excited, but he stayed very quiet.

That is, Gilbert was quiet until he and Anita got downstairs. Then he rushed to his mother and father shouting,

"I'm a mother! I'm a mother! I can feed baby birds!"

A Underline the right answers.

1. Where did the birds make their nests?

   a. on a tree

   b. on a window sill

   c. by a big rock

2. What did Anita mash for food?

   a. bread, seeds, and cereal

   b. cereal, seeds, and pizza

   c. flowers, seeds, and bread

3. When did this story happen?

   a. when it was very cold

   b. one warm spring day

   c. on a very rainy day

4. Why did Gilbert say, "I am a mother!"?

   a. He told Anita what to do.

   b. He knew how to be quiet.

   c. He thought mothers always fed babies.

5. What did Gilbert do to be quiet?

   a. He turned off the TV.

   b. He put his hand over his mouth.

   c. He locked the door.

6. How did Gilbert find out about the birds?

   a. He saw some feathers.

   b. He followed Anita.

   c. He heard the birds sing.

7. What is the best name for this story?

   a. A Room with a Lock

   b. Dad Feeds the Birds

   c. Gilbert and Anita Make New Friends

1. When did Anita forget to shut the window?

   a. What day was it? _____

   b. What month was it? _____

   c. Was it warm or cold? _____

   d. Now here is a thought question. Why do you think Anita forgot to shut the window?

   _____

   _____

2. The next day Anita went back to her secret room.

   a. What day would that be? _____

   b. What did she find there? _____

   c. Where were the birds? _____

3. Day after day, Anita saw wonderful sights.

   a. How many eggs did the birds lay? _____

   b. How long did it take for babies to come out of

     the eggs? _____

4. When did Anita make baby bird food?

   _____

   _____

   _____

a. What is that part of the day? Circle the right one.

afternoon   morning   evening

b. Why did she make the food at that time?

_____

_____

5. Where was the secret room? Circle the right one.

    a. second floor   b. first floor   c. third floor

C **What do you think happened after Gilbert told their parents
what he and Anita had been doing? Read these endings.
Put a ✔ by the ones you think could happen. Put an X by
the ones that could not happen.**

_____ 1. The family ate bird food for dinner.

_____ 2. Mom moved the birds and nest into the kitchen.

_____ 3. Mom and Dad went to see the nest.

_____ 4. The parents let the children keep on feeding the babies.

_____ 5. The birds learned to talk.

_____ 6. The birds gave food to Anita and Gilbert.

_____ 7. Gilbert frightened the birds away.

_____ 8. The baby birds got bigger and bigger.

_____ 9. Anita learned to trust her little brother.

_____ 10. The door of the secret room was locked,
        and the children never went in again.

Write the word that goes with the meaning in each egg.

a. secret   b. wonderful   c. lock
d. quiet   e. always   f. building
g. frighten   h. hungry   i. shut

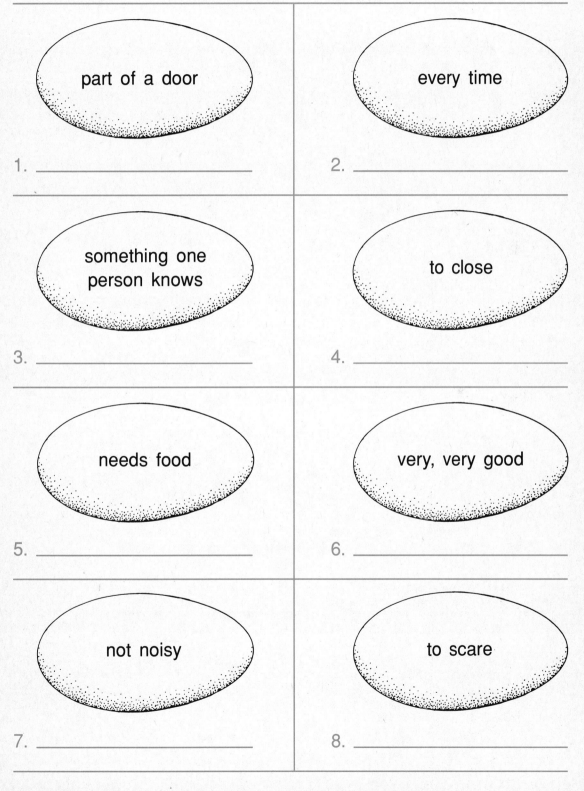

part of a door

every time

1. _____

2. _____

something one
person knows

to close

3. _____

4. _____

needs food

very, very good

5. _____

6. _____

not noisy

to scare

7. _____

8. _____

On Tuesday, some of Daisy's classmates asked, "Did you bring your check?"

"What check?" asked Daisy.

It was time to get back to work. No one had time to answer Daisy.

On the way home that afternoon, Daisy met her friend, Detective Sharp Eye. Daisy began to cry as she told him that she needed a check.

"What kind of check?" asked the detective.

Daisy whispered, "I don't know. I didn't understand."

"Let's try this check," said Mr. Sharp Eye. He gave Daisy a piece of pink paper. He made a big ✔ on it.

On Wednesday morning, Daisy was happy when she gave the teacher the check. Ms. Boone was <u>not</u> happy!

On the way home, Daisy met Detective Sharp Eye again.

"Let's see what kind of check Ms. Boone wants," he said. "We know it is not a check like the one on the pink paper. Do you think it is a check like the ones on my cap? Or, can it be some checkers?"

Daisy didn't know, so they went to ask Ms. Boone.

Ms. Boone looked surprised. "Daisy, you need a check to pay for the trip to see the pandas," she said.

"Now we understand," said Detective Sharp Eye. "When we talk about checks, we must know what kind of check is needed."

This is the check Daisy's mom gave her.

PAY TO THE ORDER OF	Ms. Boone	————— 19 — $ 4.86
	Four and 86/100	_____ DOLLARS
USA BANK		Kim Rivers

A **Underline** the right answer.

1. Why did Daisy cry?

   a. She had too many checks.

   b. She lost her check.

   c. She didn't have a check.

PAY TO THE
ORDER OF   Ms. Boone   ——— 19 —
                            $ 4.86

Four and ⁸⁶/₁₀₀   DOLLARS

USA BANK   Kim Rivers

2. What is this story about?

   a. a girl who did not see the pandas

   b. a girl who lost something

   c. a girl who didn't understand

3. Why did Daisy need help?

   a. Her mother did not have any checks.

   b. She did not know what kind of check to get.

   c. She always tripped.

4. Who was trying to help Daisy?

   a. a girl in her class

   b. a boy in her class

   c. a detective

5. What happened first?

   a. Daisy's check on pink paper

   b. the trip to see the pandas

   c. the check Daisy's mother gave her

6. Why did the class need the checks?

   a. to see if their work was good

   b. to pay for a trip to the zoo

   c. to get new caps

7. What was Detective Sharp Eye trying to teach Daisy?

   a. Words must be spelled right.

   b. She could not understand Ms. Boone's words.

   c. A word can have many meanings.

8. What surprised Ms. Boone about Daisy?

　　a. that Daisy was Detective Sharp Eye's friend

　　b. that Daisy did not know about the check

　　c. that Daisy had checks on her coat

B **Detective Sharp Eye says, "Words can have many meanings." Draw a line from the picture to the correct sentence.**

1.　　　　　　　　　　　　　　a. They have checked pants.

2.　　　　　　　　　　　　　　b. He checks a number in the telephone book.

3.　　　　　　　　　　　　　　c. She checks the children's work.

4.　　　　　　　　　　　　　　d. They play checkers.

5.　　　　　　　　　　　　　　e. She pays with a check.

Detective Sharp Eye says, "If you read carefully, you can tell who wrote these letters. Good luck!" Write the name from the box under the letter.

Ms. Boone	Pam Panda
Mr. Sharp Eye	Daisy Rivers

1. Dear Mrs. Rivers,

    Last week I met Daisy after school. She needed help again. She couldn't find her homework. I told her to think about all of the places she had been that day. She did find her homework that way. Someday she will be a good detective, too.

    Your friend,

    _____

2. Dear Mrs. Rivers,

    Daisy has been working very hard. She did very well on her math test.

    She told the class all about pandas when we went to the zoo. The class learned a lot from her.

    I hope Daisy keeps up the good work.

    Yours,

    _____

3. Dear Mr. Zookeeper,

    Why are all these people looking at us? They talk to us. They want to feed us. They will not let us sleep. If this keeps up, we will hide every day during visiting hours.

    Yours,

    _____

Circle the letter of the right meaning for each underlined word.

1. Daisy's <u>classmates</u> knew about the trip.

    a. brothers and sisters

    b. the children in her room at school

    c. the children in the city

2. Daisy was afraid that she would <u>trip</u>.

    a. go away   b. forget   c. fall

3. The class took a <u>trip</u>.

    a. fell down

    b. checked their work

    c. went somewhere

4. Mr. Sharp Eye <u>forgot</u> his lunch.

    a. took it home

    b. ate all of it

    c. did not remember to bring it

5. Mother <u>needed</u> a new checkbook.

    a. had to have   b. did not want   c. had to go away

6. "Did you bring the check?" <u>questioned</u> the teacher.

    a. asked   b. answered   c. laughed

E **Circle the best name for each story.**

1. One evening, a man came to the door. He had long whiskers and he talked funny. The children were afraid of him. They did not let him into the house. The man laughed and took off the whiskers. It was only Uncle Billy trying to be funny.

    a. The Funny Whiskers

    b. The Funny Whispers

    c. The Sad Woman

2. Our teacher, Miss Blue, always knows what we are doing. She seems to know what we are thinking, too! One day, I was mad at Tommy. I didn't tell anyone, but Miss Blue knew. She said, "Stay after school and help me. That will be better than fighting."

        a. Miss Blue Forgets Something

        b. Tommy Stops a Fight

        c. How Did She Know?

3. Sue was at the pond. A big bee buzzed around her. Sue ran away. The bee flew after her. It swooped down onto Sue's nose. Sue stood very still. She was afraid.

        a. A New Friend

        b. A Bee Lands on a Flower

        c. A Bee Lands on a Nose

F   **Detective Sharp Eye says, "If you understand all the words in a sentence, you will know what the sentence means."**
<u>Underline</u> the sentence that has the closest meaning to the first one.

1. The child gave the teacher a check.

    a. The child gave the teacher flowers.

    b. The child gave the teacher money.

    c. The child gave the teacher nothing.

2. Daisy and her class took a trip.

    a. They went away.

    b. They fell down.

    c. Daisy fell down.

3. Daisy followed her friends.

    a. She walked after them.

    b. She walked before them.

    c. She went the other way.

4

One Thursday evening in May, Ann and Jeff had a cookout in their front yard. Jeff asked three of his friends to come. Ann asked four children from her class to come.

The cookout started at five o'clock. Dad cooked hot dogs and hamburgers over a grill. Mom cooked potatoes and corn, too. The children ate until they were full!

"Now it is time for the treasure hunt!" Ann yelled.

"The one who finds the treasure box can keep it!"

Jeff led the children to the side yard. They hunted for the treasure box. No one found it.

They ran on to the back yard. Ann's friend, Ed, found the treasure box. It was hidden between two rocks near the oak tree.

The treasure box was full of tiny toys for everyone to take home. The girls picked out small red, white, and blue drums. The boys wanted the little orange horns. Ed got to keep the treasure box and a horn.

Then Mom had a big surprise! She had little ice creams in the shape of flowers for everyone. At seven o'clock the children finished eating their ice cream and went home.

A **<u>Underline</u> the right answer.**

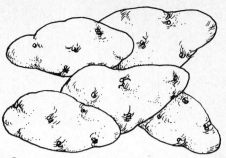

1. What was this story about?

   a. cooking out on the sand

   b. a cookout at someone's house

   c. a cookout at school

2. Which food did they eat at the cookout?

   a. cake   b. corn   c. candy

3. How many boys were at this cookout?

   a. four

   b. five

   c. The story did not tell.

4. Where did the children hunt first?

   a. in the side yard

   b. in the back yard

   c. The story did not tell.

5. When did they eat ice cream?

   a. before seven o'clock

   b. before five o'clock

   c. after seven o'clock

6. Where was the treasure box?

   a. between some rocks

   b. under some rocks

   c. up in an oak tree

7. Which treasure do you think Mary got?

   a. a drum   b. a horn   c. a treasure box

8. What is the best name for this story?

   a. A Day of Fun

   b. An Evening of Fun

   c. The Picnic in the Park

B Dear Friends,
 Be a smart detective like me. Here
 are some hard questions. Put your
 clues together and solve the mystery.
 Good luck!

 Detective Sharp Eye

1. How many children were at the cookout? Use these steps and your story to find out.

 a. First, circle the faces of the children who gave the cookout.

  How many did you circle? _____

 b. Next, check off the number of children Jeff asked to the

  cookout. How many did Jeff ask? _____

 c. Now check off the number of children Ann asked to the

  cookout. How many did Ann ask? _____

 d. Cross out any faces you did not need.

 e. Now add the numbers to tell how many children were at the

  cookout. _____ children were there.

2. How long did the cookout last? Look for clues in the story.
 Here is how Detective Sharp Eye worked it out!

 a. Tell the time the cookout started. _____

 b. Tell the time the cookout ended. _____

 c. Now you can tell how long the cookout lasted. _____ hours

24

3. Ed found the treasure box. Which child is sharp-eyed Ed? Read the clues about these three boys to find out.

_____   _____   _____

      Jeff is a tall boy who likes to play ball. He has asked his friends to the cookout.

      Ed likes to play baseball. Ed's team always plays on Thursday afternoons.

      Tommy likes to play ball games with Ed and Jeff. Tommy is not a tall boy. He is shorter than Jeff and Ed.

a. Write each boy's name under his picture.
b. Put a big box around Ed's picture.

4. What did the children eat at the cookout? Look in the story. Can you tell every food they ate?

_____   _____

_____   _____

_____

5. Did the children like the food? Write the sentence from the story which tells if the children liked the food.

_____

6. Where were the hot dogs cooked? They were cooked on a

_____ .

7. What did the ice cream look like?

Write the word. _____
Use the space at the right to draw
the shape of the ice cream they ate.

C Can you put the right word in each sentence?

treasure	cookout	class	shape
hamburger	between	grill	potato

1. A _____ is a meal fixed outdoors.

2. They cut the brown skin off the white _____.

3. Some ground meat on a roll is called a _____.

4. We use a _____ to cook meat over a fire.

5. A very good thing that everyone wants is a _____.

6. The ice cream was cut in the _____ of flowers.

7. Children in Jeff's room at school are in his _____.

D (Circle) the right word to end the sentence.

1. Father made a fire. Then he put the hot dogs on the _____ to cook.

   a. ground   b. grill   c. grass

2. The hamburgers were ready to eat. They smelled so good. Each child put a hamburger on a _____.

   a. rug   b. rock   c. roll

3. Ed looked near the oak tree. He found a box. He opened it and found a _____ in it.

   a. treetop   b. treasure   c. through

4. Ed found the treasure _____ two big rocks.

   a. between   b. belong   c. became

5. Ann asked some friends in her _____ to the cookout.

   a. class   b. climb   c. clock

6. The sun goes down and it gets dark in the _____.

   a. every   b. even   c. evening

7. The hamburger rolls were the same _____ as the meat.

   a. shake   b. shape   c. shell

Let's have a treasure hunt. Ed found the treasure. Follow his tracks and find the treasure. Can you answer the questions?

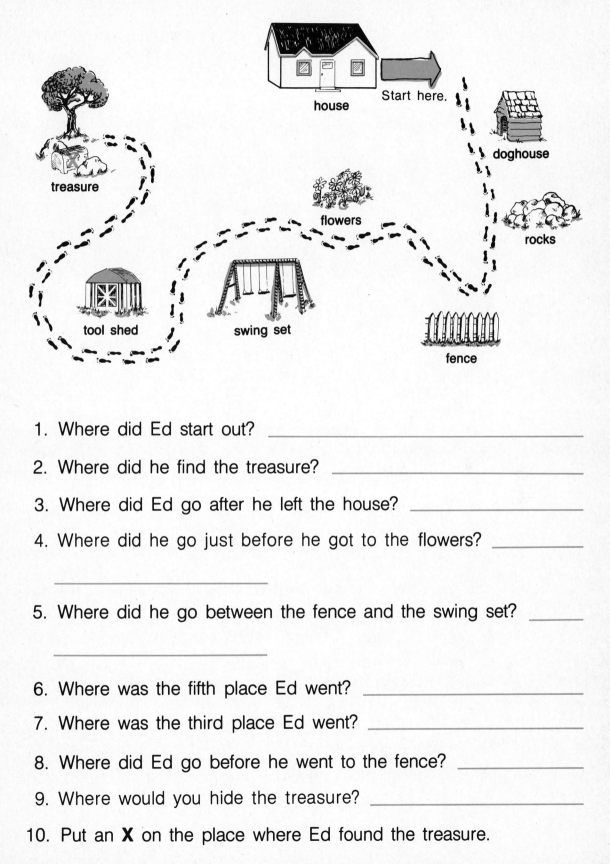

1. Where did Ed start out? _____

2. Where did he find the treasure? _____

3. Where did Ed go after he left the house? _____

4. Where did he go just before he got to the flowers? _____

   _____

5. Where did he go between the fence and the swing set? _____

   _____

6. Where was the fifth place Ed went? _____

7. Where was the third place Ed went? _____

8. Where did Ed go before he went to the fence? _____

9. Where would you hide the treasure? _____

10. Put an **X** on the place where Ed found the treasure.

① Lee played on the beach one morning. He walked near the water. His feet felt wet and cold, but it was a hot July day.

② The sea came up on the sand. It splashed on Lee's feet. Then the water went back out again. Every time the sea went out, it left water plants all over the sand. It left many kinds of shells on the sand, too.

③ Lee found some shells and put them in his bag. The sea came splashing up on the sand again. Lee picked up a beautiful pink shell. He had never seen a shell like this one before. Then Lee saw a friend walking over to him.

④ "That is a very pretty shell," said Lee's friend. "That kind of shell is hard to find. If you will sell it to me, I will pay you ten dollars."

⑤ Lee did not know what to do. He liked the shell, but he wanted the money, too. Then he thought that the sea might bring him another beautiful shell some day soon. Lee sold the shell.

A **Underline the right answer.**

1. What is this story about?

   a. Lee found something good.

   b. Lee lost something.

   c. A friend found what Lee had lost.

2. When did Lee play on the beach?

   a. one afternoon in June

   b. one July morning

   c. on a May evening

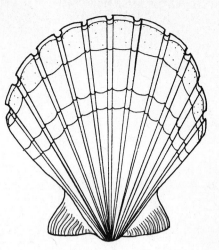

3. Where did this happen?

   a. on a boat

   b. near the sea

   c. in a garden

4. Why were Lee's feet so cold and wet?

   a. The sea was splashing them.

   b. It was raining.

   c. He walked in the pond.

5. What did Lee get for the shell?

   a. ten dollars

   b. nothing

   c. two dollars

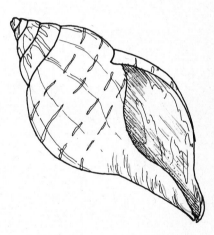

6. Why did Lee's friend want the shell?

   a. It was not like other shells.

   b. The shell had a fish in it.

   c. He wanted to play with it.

7. When did Lee's friend give Lee some money?

   a. before Lee found the shell

   b. after Lee found the shell

   c. He never gave Lee any money.

8. What is the best name for this story?

   a. The Sea Went Out Again

   b. A Sandy Story

   c. Lee Sells Something

B This story has five parts called **paragraphs**. Each paragraph has a number beside it. Detective Sharp Eye wants you to find these things.

1. Write the first word in paragraph ③. _____

2. Write the third word in paragraph ②. _____

3. Write the last word in paragraph ⑤. _____

4. Write the last word in paragraph ④. _____

5. Write the second word in paragraph ①. _____

C Are you a good detective? Write the number of the paragraph that tells:

1. the kind of day it was _____

2. how much money Lee got from his friend _____

3. what Lee picked up _____

4. the color of the shell _____

5. if Lee sold the shell _____

6. what splashed on Lee's feet _____

D What is each paragraph about? Look at the story again. Use the words in the box.

Lee	the sea	a friend

1. Paragraph ① is about _____.

2. Paragraph ④ is about _____.

3. Paragraph ③ is about _____.

4. Paragraph ⑤ is about _____.

5. Paragraph ② is about _____.

E **Which picture goes with the paragraph? Write the letter of the right picture next to the paragraph that tells about it.**

1. _____ The sea water splashed up on the sand. It left many things there. It left plants and shells on the sand.

2. _____ Far out on the blue sea was a big boat. The boat was sailing along fast. It was going away from the sand.

3. _____ Some people were walking along the sand. Their feet were getting wet. Other people were swimming and splashing in the deep water.

4. _____ Under the water, many fish were swimming. Some were very big fish. Others were very small. Some fish were swimming together in a school.

5. _____ Then rain started to fall. People came out of the water. Raindrops made the sand wet.

F Use your sharp eyes to find the two sentences in this paragraph that do not belong. Cross them out. Then write the paragraph again. Write only the sentences you did not cross out.

The sea is very big. Many animals live in the sea. Many plants live there, too. A rainbow has many colors. The sea leaves plants and shells on the sand. There are many plants and animals in a forest.

_____

_____

_____

_____

_____

G Write the letter for each word next to the right meaning.

a. dollars   b. thought   c. beautiful   d. morning
e. another   f. splash   g. July   h. every

_____ 1. a summer month   _____ 2. one more

_____ 3. a noise water makes   _____ 4. some money

_____ 5. very pretty   _____ 6. did think

H Find the last part of each sentence. Write the letter of the last part on the line next to the first part of the sentence.

_____ 1. People hunt for shells   a. it must be night.

_____ 2. If you want to buy   b. on the sand by the sea.
           something,
                                       c. your feet will get wet.

_____ 3. If it is sunny outside,
                                       d. you must have some money.

_____ 4. If it is dark outside,
                                       e. it cannot be night yet.

_____ 5. If you walk into
           water,   f. your feet will not get wet.

32

I **How good are your eyes? Look at the picture. Then answer the questions.**

1. How many fish can you find in the picture? _____

2. What is all around the plants and animals? _____

3. How many people do you see in the picture? _____

4. How many snakes do you find here? _____

5. How many shells and rocks are there? _____

6. How many times a day must you water these plants? _____

7. Do you see three seals in the picture? _____

8. Are there any rocks in the picture? _____

9. Where is the longest fish swimming?
   (on the top, middle, or bottom) _____

A **Read this story and answer the questions.**

Milly and Ron rode their bikes to the store. They needed to buy some food for lunch. They were very careful on their bikes.

When they got to the store, Ron stayed outside to watch the bikes. Milly went inside the store to buy the food.

Milly looked all around the store for the things she needed. She got bread, hamburger meat, milk, and ice cream. Milly paid for the food and left the store. Then she and Ron rode home.

1. How many paragraphs are in this story? _____

2. Write the last word in the second paragraph. _____

3. Write the sixth word in the third paragraph. _____

4. Write the last word in the first paragraph. _____

5. Write the tenth word in the first paragraph. _____

6. What are the children's names? _____ _____

7. How did the children get to the store? Circle the answer.
   a. They walked.   b. They rode bikes.   c. They took a bus.

8. Why did Ron stay outside the store? Circle the answer.
   a. He watched the bikes.
   b. He could not go inside.
   c. He wanted to stay in the sun.

9. Name all the foods Milly got at the store. _____

_____   _____   _____

10. Paragraph _____ has a sentence that tells when Ron and Milly were going to eat the food.

11. Paragraph _____ tells how careful they were on bikes.

12. Paragraph _____ tells the kinds of food that Milly got.

13. Paragraph _____ is about riding to the store.

14. Paragraph _____ is about buying the food and going home.

15. Paragraph _____ tells who stayed outside the store.

16. The story does not tell us how Ron and Milly carried the food home. But a good detective can learn how they did it. Look back at page 34 for a clue to answer these questions.

   a. How do you think Milly and Ron carried the food home?

   _____

   b. What is the clue that you used? _____

B **Can you write a paragraph? Use four of the sentences below. First, pick the sentence that will start the paragraph. Next, cross out one sentence that does not belong in the paragraph. Last, write your paragraph on the lines below.**

1. They ate hamburgers and then ate ice cream.
2. The children got a letter from Grandmother.
3. Milly and Ron knew how to fix lunch.
4. First, Milly put the bread and plates on the table.
5. Then, Ron cooked the hamburger in a pan.

_____

_____

_____

_____

_____

Detective Sharp Eye wants you to find the picture that goes with each story. Look for clues in the story.

Two children found a treasure. It was a gold horse. The galloping horse had a mane but not reins. Circle the treasure.

1. a.   b.   c.

The two brothers had a small bedroom. One bed was on top of the other bed. The boys liked to sleep in their bunk beds. Find their bedroom. Circle it.

2. a.   b.   c.

The bookworm often stopped in the classroom to take a bite out of the reading books. These books were very sweet and good to eat. One day the bookworm had just taken a bite of a paragraph. A woman came through the door. The woman picked up the book and shut it quickly. Only the bookworm's head was left out of the book. Put a check on the picture that shows what happened.

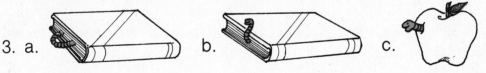

3. a.   b.   c.

Two girls were sitting at a table. They were playing a game. One girl moved a red circle. The other girl moved a black circle over the top of the red circle. What game were they playing? Circle the game.

4. a.   b.   c.

Mrs. Rivers has a new job. She is a mounted police officer. Put a check on her picture.

5. a.   b.   c.

D The pandas are in a line. Mark them as the sentences tell you.

1. Circle the second panda.
2. Put an **X** on the middle panda.
3. Underline the third panda and the sixth one.
4. Color the seventh panda yellow.
5. Put a dot on the third panda.
6. Make a star under the fifth and sixth pandas.
7. Put a ✔ over the first and last pandas.

E Draw a line from each sentence to the right picture.

a.

1. I will park the truck.
2. The zoo is in the park.

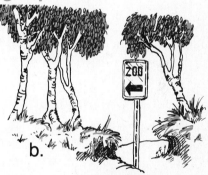

b.

3. The jacket has checks on it.
4. Daisy put checks on the paper.

c.

d.

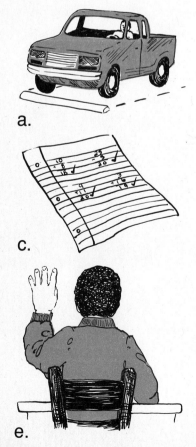

5. This is my left hand.
6. We left the car.

e.

f.

37

F (Circle) the meaning of the underlined word. Be sure the meaning makes sense.

1. Ms. Boone told Daisy to <u>hand</u> the papers to her classmates.

   a. part of Daisy

   b. give out

   c. take back

2. Jan is the <u>last</u> in line.

   a. the second one

   b. the first one

   c. the end one

3. The boots <u>lasted</u> all winter.

   a. were good for a long time

   b. were not good

   c. were at the end of the line

4. Ricky gave the cat some <u>water</u>.

   a. a place for a boat

   b. something to drink

   c. a brook

G Fill in the blanks, using the words in the box. Each word may be used more than once.

light	check	back

1. Please _____ your homework so it will be right.

2. Dan's pants are _____ brown.

3. Ann can pick up the big box. It is _____.

4. Daisy went _____ to school at eleven o'clock.

5. We will write a _____ to pay the bill.

H **Read each story. Circle the best name.**

1. Two baby birds got bigger. One baby was tiny. The bigger babies wanted all the food. Anita saw this. So she always put food in the smallest baby's bill. Soon the tiny one got big, too.

   a. Anita Helps a Bird

   b. What Birds Eat

   c. A Bird Helps Anita

2. Two workers took Mike out of his stall. They washed him. They brushed his hair. They looked at his horseshoes. Another person cleaned Mike's stall.

   a. New Horseshoes

   b. The Horse Gallops

   c. Taking Care of Mike

I **Write the correct word in each blank.**

rains	reins	checks	mane	main

1. What is the _____ part of the story?

2. When it _____, the streets get wet.

3. She holds the _____ to control the horse.

4. The hair on a horse's neck is a _____.

5. Mom writes _____ to pay the bills.

6. The heavy _____ bring water to the plants.

7. The shirt had red and blue _____ on it.

8. The officer brushed his horse's _____.

9. The rider must hold the horse's _____ to stay on.

1 Wally Bluewhale was just a baby. But Wally was bigger than a bus! Wally was a whale, and whales are bigger than other animals.

2 At first, Wally stayed near his mother. They swam together in the sea. Wally had to learn all the things a baby whale must learn. Learning was fun for Wally!

3 Learning to eat was fun. Mother Bluewhale showed Wally how to open his mouth and swim right through a lot of tiny fish and water plants. As he swam through, the tiny fish and water plants just popped into his mouth. Yum! Yum! Good!

4 Learning to play was fun, too. Whales cannot stay under water like fish. Whales must go up to the top of the water for air. They made a big game of it. Mother and the other whales splashed out of the water and jumped up in the air! They had fun!

5 Wally went with them! Bang! His tail hit the water. He liked to hear the noise. He rolled over on his back. He rolled over to his front. He let a big spray of water splash out of his head.

6 Wally looked at his neighbors in the sea around him. He saw an octopus hiding in the rocks. He saw a big fish eating tiny fish. He saw a turtle hiding in its shell.

7 "Wow!" said Wally as he rolled over. "I'm so lucky! I'm happy to be me—a big blue whale!"

A Underline the right answer.

1. What is one thing we learned about Wally?

   a. He ate big fish.

   b. He was not happy.

   c. He was a happy animal.

2. Why did Wally think he was lucky?

   a. He had to leave the sea.

   b. He found some money in the sea.

   c. He did not have to be afraid of other animals.

3. How do baby whales learn?

   a. by reading a book

   b. by seeing what big whales do

   c. People show them how to do things.

4. Why do whales go to the top of the water?

   a. to play

   b. to eat bugs

   c. to take in air

5. What would happen if Wally did not go to the top of the water?

   a. He would not live.

   b. Nothing would happen.

   c. He would not learn.

6. What can Wally the whale do?

   a. walk on land

   b. sit in a sailboat

   c. spray water from his head

7. What is the best name for this story?

   a. The Lucky Octopus

   b. A Playful Animal

   c. A Careful Animal

B This story has seven paragraphs. Each paragraph has a number before it. Detective Sharp Eye wants you to use the numbers to find these things.

1. Write the first word in paragraph ⑦. _____

2. Write the third word in paragraph ④. _____

3. Write the last word in paragraph ⑦. _____

4. Write the fifth word in paragraph ③. _____

5. Write the eighth word in paragraph ⑤. _____

6. Which paragraph does not have the name *Wally* in it? _____

C Are you a good detective?  Which paragraph tells about each of these things? Write the number of the right paragraph in the blank.

_____ 1. whale games

_____ 2. how big Wally was

_____ 3. Wally's food

_____ 4. Wally's neighbors

_____ 5. going up for air

_____ 6. Wally banging his tail

_____ 7. how to eat water plants

_____ 8. how Wally felt about himself

_____ 9. Wally staying near his mother

_____ 10. Wally spraying water from his head

_____ 11. learning to play

_____ 12. what the turtle was doing

D **Can you put the right word in each sentence?**

lucky	learn	through
noise	game	small
hiding	spray	together
	bigger	

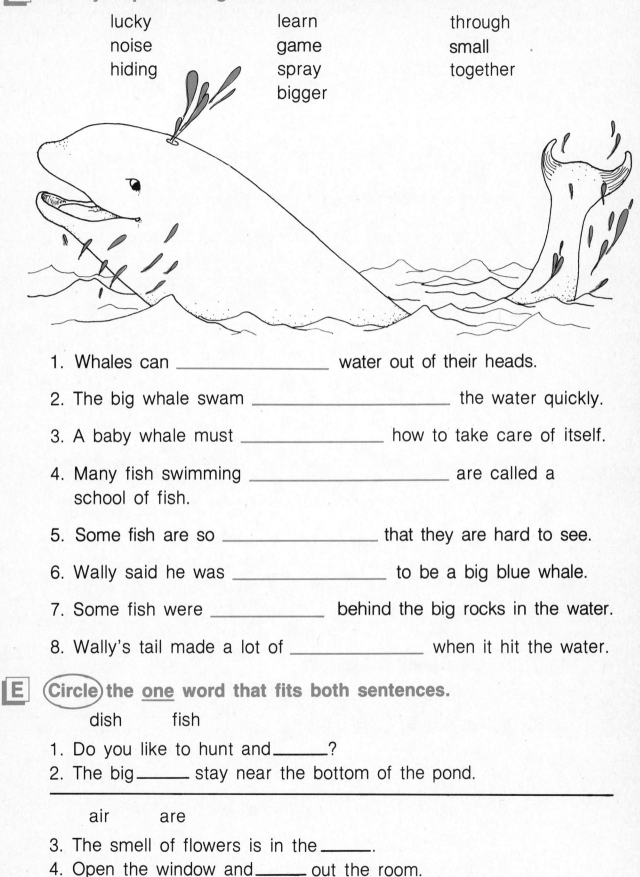

1. Whales can _____ water out of their heads.

2. The big whale swam _____ the water quickly.

3. A baby whale must _____ how to take care of itself.

4. Many fish swimming _____ are called a school of fish.

5. Some fish are so _____ that they are hard to see.

6. Wally said he was _____ to be a big blue whale.

7. Some fish were _____ behind the big rocks in the water.

8. Wally's tail made a lot of _____ when it hit the water.

E (Circle) the <u>one</u> word that fits both sentences.

dish   fish

1. Do you like to hunt and_____?
2. The big_____ stay near the bottom of the pond.

air   are

3. The smell of flowers is in the_____.
4. Open the window and_____ out the room.

F Can you write a paragraph? Use four of the sentences below. One sentence does not fit the name of the paragraph. Read the name carefully.

1. Whales are afraid of people.
2. There are many kinds of whales.
3. People kill many whales every year.
4. Whales are not afraid of other animals.
5. Other animals do not kill whales.

What Whales Are Afraid Of

_____

_____

_____

_____

_____

_____

_____

G There is a mark at the end of each sentence that means to stop. A sentence that **asks** you something has a **?** at the end. A sentence that **tells** you something has a **.** at the end. A sentence that shows that you are **mad**, **happy**, or **afraid** has an **!** at the end. Put a **.** or a **?** or an **!** at the end of each sentence.

1. Swim fast or they will kill us

2. Did you ever see a whale walking

3. A whale is bigger than a truck

4. Do whales come up to the top of the water for air

5. Wow, I'm so lucky to be me

6. The grass will get green if you spray water on it

7. Help me

8. Is this your lucky day

44

What do you think will happen next? Put a ✔ by it.

1. Some people were hunting for whales. They were going to kill the whales and sell them. Wally Bluewhale saw the hunters in a boat. What do you think Wally did?

_____ a. Wally swam into the side of the boat and made the boat go down.

_____ b. Wally swam far down near the bottom of the sea to hide.

2. Whales swam through the water. They heard a noise and went to see what it was. They came too near land. They got stuck on the land. What do you think happened to the whales?

_____ a. People had to help the whales get back into the water.

_____ b. The whales got up and walked back into the water.

3. A baby whale got stuck in an old boat at the bottom of the sea. Baby Whale could not get out. Mother Whale had to help Baby Whale quickly. What did Baby Whale have to do after Mother Whale helped him get out of the old boat?

_____ a. Baby Whale had to get back in the boat.

_____ b. Baby Whale had to go up to the top of the water to get some air.

4. The whales had been swimming and playing in the sea. It was time to eat and they were hungry. The whales swam to a place where there were many small fish and water plants. What do you think the whales did?

_____ a. The whales opened their mouths.

_____ b. The whales swam to another place in the sea.

This was the second time that Jan and Dan were going to camp for two weeks. Last year they had a good time at Camp Oak Tree.

They came to the camp on Saturday morning. Jan and Dan were happy to see their old friends from last year. It was fun to move into the little bunkhouses. They splashed in the lake. Later they ate dinner around the campfire.

Sunday and Monday were beautiful days. Everyone was happy and busy. They played, read, swam, rode horses, and made things.

On Tuesday, things started to happen to make this year different at Camp Oak Tree. It rained hard and long! The bunkhouses had water all over the floors by evening.

The fifth day was sunny. But the children had to mop up the water. They cleaned up the mess until late afternoon.

On Thursday, they went for a long ride on horses. At noon they were ready to eat lunch, but the cook's helpers forgot to bring the food!

The seventh day, some bees came to stay in a tree by the big house. Dan and Jan walked under the tree that morning. The bees buzzed at Dan and stung Jan! But they still had fun that afternoon going on boat rides on the lake.

On Saturday morning, many people who worked at the camp got sick. They could not take care of the children. That afternoon, fathers and mothers came and took all the children home.

Jan said, "Dan, next year will be better! We'll be back!"

A **<u>Underline</u> the right answer.**

1. How long did Jan and Dan stay at camp this year?

    a. two weeks   b. one month   c. one week

2. When had Dan and Jan been to camp before?

    a. last month   b. last year   c. last week

3. How did Jan and Dan get home from camp?

    a. They walked home.

    b. Their mother and father came to get them.

    c. They rode in a big bus.

4. What did Dan and Jan do on Wednesday?

    a. They cleaned up the water.

    b. They rode horses all day.

    c. They took boat rides on the lake.

5. Why did water cover the floors of the bunkhouses?

    a. Children forgot to turn the water off.

    b. It rained too much at one time.

    c. The children learned how to swim that way.

6. What came first?

    a. cleaning up the mess

    b. going on boat rides

    c. getting stung by a bee

7. What would have happened if no one had become sick?

    a. The children would have stayed one more day.

    b. The children would have stayed one more month.

    c. The children would have stayed one more week.

8. What is the best name for this story?

    a. Dan and Jan at Camp Oak Tree

    b. Camping Out in the Woods

    c. Bees Come to Camp Oak Tree

B Fill in the missing days and times. These lists will help you!

Days of the Week

1. Sunday   5. Thursday
2. Monday   6. Friday
3. Tuesday   7. Saturday
4. Wednesday

Times of the Day

1. morning   4. evening
2. noon   5. night
3. afternoon 6. midnight

1. Thursday, _____, Saturday

2. Sunday, _____, Tuesday, _____

3. Wednesday, _____, _____

4. _____, Saturday, _____, Monday

5. _____, _____, Thursday

6. noon, afternoon, _____, night

7. _____, noon, afternoon, evening, _____

8. _____, midnight, morning, _____

C Here is part of a calendar. Can you mark the days when these things happened?

JULY

Sunday	Monday	Tuesday	Wednesday	Thursday	Friday	Saturday
						7
8	9	10	11	12	13	14
15						

1. Put a purple ✔ on the day the children had to mop up water.
2. Put a green dot on the second day they were at camp.
3. Make a tiny orange box on the day they had to go home.
4. Make a big yellow sun on the day they got to Camp Oak Tree.
5. Put two drops of rain on the day it rained all day.
6. Draw a bee on the day Jan got stung by a bee.
7. Make a circle around the day no one ate lunch.
8. Put a black **M** on the day some people got sick.

When did this happen? A smart detective will check back in the story. Then (circle) the right answer.

1. a. Saturday morning
   b. Wednesday morning

2. a. Sunday morning
   b. Thursday morning

3. a. all day on Tuesday
   b. Monday morning

4. a. Friday at noon
   b. Saturday evening

5. a. early on Friday
   b. late Friday night

6. a. Friday afternoon
   b. early Sunday morning

E **Read this story to find out how long each child stayed at camp.**

All the children came to summer camp on a big bus.

Sandy stayed at the camp on Saturday, Sunday, Monday, Tuesday, Wednesday, Thursday, Friday, Saturday, Sunday, Monday, Tuesday, Wednesday, Thursday, and Friday.

Beth was there on Saturday, Sunday, Monday, Tuesday, Wednesday, Thursday, and Friday. Then she went home.

Jay missed his mother and dad. He wanted to be back at home. Jay only stayed Saturday, Sunday, Monday, Tuesday, and Wednesday.

Les was at camp on Saturday, Sunday, Monday, Tuesday, Wednesday, Thursday, and Friday.

Write a letter under each picture to tell how long each child stayed at camp.

    a. less than one week   b. one week
    c. more than one week   d. two weeks

    Les   Beth   Jay   Sandy

1. _____   2. _____   3. _____   4. _____

F **Draw lines to match these.**

1. place to sleep at camp   week

2. place to walk on   forgot

3. seven days   bunkhouse

4. hurt by a bee   campfire

5. not like others   camp

6. did not take   stung

7. a place to stay away from home   floor

                                                    different

50

G When Cathy and Jimmy went to camp, they wrote to their mom and dad. Read about their camp. Then read their letters. Which day were they telling about? Write the name of the day on the line.

On Sunday, they had a funny clown show. The next day they had a rock hunt. The kids put a frog in Sue's bed on Tuesday.

Jimmy had a cold on Wednesday. That day Cathy went on a long ride on a horse to Big Rock. The next day everyone cooked hot dogs around the campfire and sang songs.

Cathy lost her tennis shoes on Friday. Jimmy found some money the next day.

1. Hi!
　　Today we found a frog by the lake. We put it in Sue's bed! You could hear her yell for a long way!

Love,

_____ Cathy

2. Dear Mom and Dad,
　　My brother was sick today, but I rode to Big Rock on a horse. I am riding much better now.

Love,

_____ Cathy

3. Hello!
　　The food here was bad today. After dinner we saw a clown show. It was so funny!

Love,

_____ Jimmy

4. Dear Family,
　　I am taking care of my things, but Cathy is not. She lost her tennis shoes today.

Love,

_____ Jimmy

5. Dear Mom and Dad,
　　We were going to ask you for some money, but now we don't need it. This morning Jim found five dollars in the woods. Please send the money next week.

Thanks,

Cathy and Jimmy

_____

A mother raccoon had three hungry babies. These babies ate so much food, that they cried for food all the time.

"Eat! Eat! Eat! All they want to do is eat!" said Mother Raccoon. "As soon as they get bigger, I will teach them how to find their own food."

She waited for the right time. On a Tuesday night in July, she took them to the pond. Mother Raccoon showed the babies how to catch fish. They got nine fish for a good dinner.

The very next night, Mother Raccoon took the babies to a field of corn. They did not make noise as they crept in. Each raccoon picked an ear of corn. Then they all went to the brook. They washed the corn in the water. Again they had a good meal.

On Thursday night, the raccoon family went to a garden. The garden was in back of a farmer's house. The raccoons crept under the fence to get in. What a good meal they had there! They ate lettuce, berries, cabbage, and carrots. They ate so much that they could not get back under the fence to go home. The fat raccoons crept by the farmer's front door. Then they went out an open gate.

"We're lucky that the farmer did not see us!" said Mother.

A **Underline** the right answer.

1. Which time of year did this story happen?

   a. summer   b. winter   c. fall

2. When did the raccoons go hunting for food?

   a. daytime   b. after dark   c. before dark

3. Why did the mother teach the babies to find their own food?

   a. She did not like the babies.

   b. She wanted them to help the farmer.

   c. She wanted them to take care of themselves.

4. Where did the raccoons go on Wednesday night?

   a. to a store

   b. to a pond

   c. to a field of corn

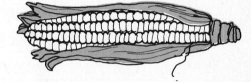

5. What do we know about the baby raccoons?

   a. They were hungry all the time.

   b. They were never hungry.

   c. They did not listen to their mother.

6. What did the raccoons do before they ate corn?

   a. They paid for it.

   b. They cleaned it in some water.

   c. They cooked it on a grill.

7. Why did the raccoons try not to make noise in the garden?

   a. They did not want to wake up the rabbits.

   b. They did not want to wake up the plants.

   c. They did not want to wake up the farmer.

8. How did the raccoons get out of the garden?

   a. They climbed over the fence.

   b. They walked past the farmer's door.

   c. They dug under the fence.

9. What is the best name for this story?

   a. The Baby Raccoons Learn Something New

   b. Mother Raccoon Learns Something New

   c. The Farmer's Big Garden

B Detective Sharp Eye wants you to put the story in the right order. Find the missing sentences in the box. Write the sentences on the lines where they belong.

> a. They got fish at the pond.
> b. They could not get under the fence again.
> c. They crept into the field of corn.
> d. They crept in to get some potatoes.

1. The raccoon babies were crying for food.
2. Mother Raccoon took them out hunting.

3. _____

4. _____

5. They crept into the farmer's garden.
6. They ate too much food.

7. _____

C Detective Sharp Eye wants you to tell when these things happened. <u>Underline</u> the right answer.

1. When did the raccoons wash and clean the corn?

   a. before they went into the field

   b. after they were in the field

2. When did the family go to the pond?

   a. before they went to the field of corn

   b. after they went to the garden

3. When did the babies cry for food?

   a. before they learned to find food

   b. after they learned to find food

4. When did they go into the farmer's garden?

   a. on Tuesday   b. on Wednesday   c. on Thursday

5. At noon, what do you think the raccoons were doing?

   a. washing food   b. sleeping   c. eating corn

54

D | Draw lines to match these.

1. animals with rings on their tails   crept

2. moved slowly   field

3. ground where corn grows   raccoons

4. needing to eat   wash

5. red fruit   cabbage

6. an orange food   hungry

7. Mother's little ones   carrot

8. to clean food   babies

           berries

E | What do you know about raccoons?

1. Which one is a raccoon? Circle it.

a.   b.   c.

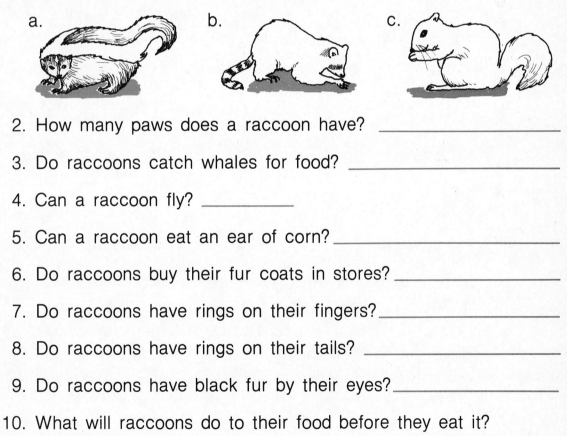

2. How many paws does a raccoon have? _____

3. Do raccoons catch whales for food? _____

4. Can a raccoon fly? _____

5. Can a raccoon eat an ear of corn? _____

6. Do raccoons buy their fur coats in stores? _____

7. Do raccoons have rings on their fingers? _____

8. Do raccoons have rings on their tails? _____

9. Do raccoons have black fur by their eyes? _____

10. What will raccoons do to their food before they eat it?

_____

11. Name six foods that raccoons will eat. _____

_____

F **Read each story. Draw a line from the question to the answer.**

Tiger Cat showed her kittens how to catch mice. The two kittens ran after a fat, gray mouse. But the mouse got away. The next time the kittens went after a mouse, they did catch it.

1. What happened first?

2. What happened next?

3. What happened last?

a. A mouse got away from the kittens.

b. Tiger Cat showed the kittens how to hunt.

c. The kittens got a mouse.

Last week, Mr. Black helped Mr. and Mrs. Fell. Their car had stopped in the street. First, Mr. Fell tried to start the car. But it would not start. Then Mrs. Fell tried to start the car. It still did not start. Mr. Black got some gas in a can for Mr. and Mrs. Fell. They put the gas in. The car started.

4. What came first?

5. What came second?

6. What came third?

7. What came last?

a. The woman could not fix the car.

b. Mr. Black got some gas for Mr. and Mrs. Fell.

c. Mr. Fell could not fix the car.

d. The car stopped in the street.

For a long time, no one wanted to play baseball with Todd. He could not catch, hit, or run fast. Then Todd's dad showed him how to be a better player. Todd and his dad worked for five weeks. One day the children needed another player. They had to let Todd play. They got a surprise! Todd hit a home run!

8. What happened first?

9. What happened second?

10. What happened third?

11. What happened last?

a. No one would let Todd play ball.

b. Todd hit a home run.

c. They let Todd play in the game.

d. Todd and Dad worked on hitting.

Mr. Raccoon's Food

Mr. Raccoon liked to eat frogs better than anything. Frogs were easy to catch in the water. He could wash frogs and eat them quickly. But this week Mr. Raccoon was not lucky. He could not catch a frog. On Monday he ate only berries. The next night Mr. Raccoon had to fight with a little garden snake before he could eat it. On Wednesday he found some bugs on a tree to eat. He ate a thin, gray mouse on Thursday.

G **Read Mr. Raccoon's story. Mr. Raccoon wrote a diary of what happened each day. Here are his diary pages and the things he wrote. Write what happened next to the right date. The first one is done for you.**

a. The frogs are still too fast for me. I had nothing to eat but some black bugs!

b. The frogs were too quick for me. So I had some berries to eat.

c. All I could catch tonight was a thin mouse. The mouse was not very much to eat.

d. The snake tried to get away. What a fight! But I got it!

1. **Sunday, August 10 —** _I want to eat some good frogs._

Tomorrow I'll try to catch some frogs.

2. **Monday, August 11 —** _____

_____

3. **Tuesday, August 12 —** _____

_____

4. **Wednesday, August 13 —** _____

_____

5. **Thursday, August 14 —** _____

_____

The people of Butterfield have a car race on the second Saturday of October every year. Each family builds a small car and one child drives it. Winter Street is a big hill where they race.

Twelve cars were in the race last October. Mr. and Mrs. Press and their children had made a yellow car. It had a big black number eight on each side. Jenny Press was going to drive it.

Pop! The gun went off and the race started! Cars rolled down the big hill. People yelled for the car they liked best.

Car number six never got started. Its brake was stuck. Soon a front wheel fell off car number nine. It could not move. Car number three ran into car number four. Both cars were out of the race.

Jenny Press kept going. She was in front of all the other cars. Jenny looked behind her to see how far back the other cars were. That made her car slow down. Quickly, Chuck Rand in car number eleven went past Jenny.

Chuck won the race and Jenny came in right after him. Next came car number one with car number seven right beside it.

"It's a tie for third place!" yelled the people who watched.

Next came car two, then car twelve, then car five. Car number ten came in last.

A   <u>Underline</u> the right answer.

1. What was the story about?

   a. horse racing in Butterfield

   b. bike racing on Winner Street

   c. car racing on Winter Street

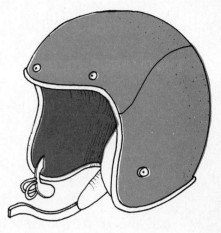

2. How often did they have this race?

   a. every year

   b. every month

   c. every week

3. What do you think Butterfield was?

   a. a big hill

   b. a school

   c. a small town

4. When was the race held?

   a. summer   b. fall   c. spring

5. How many cars finished the race?

   a. eight   b. twelve   c. four

6. Who came in first?

   a. Chuck Rand in number eleven

   b. Kevin in number one

   c. Jenny Press in number eight

7. Which car came in last?

   a. number two

   b. number ten

   c. number twelve

8. How did cars seven and one end the race?

   a. first and last

   b. at the same time

   c. They did not finish.

9. What kept Jenny from winning the race?

    a. The brake did not work.

    b. Her front wheel fell off.

    c. She looked back and slowed down.

10. What is the best name for this story?

    a. A Sled Race on Winter Hill

    b. Jenny Wins the Race

    c. Lost by a Look

B **This is a picture of the end of the race. The numbers on the cars are not clear. Put the right number on each car.**

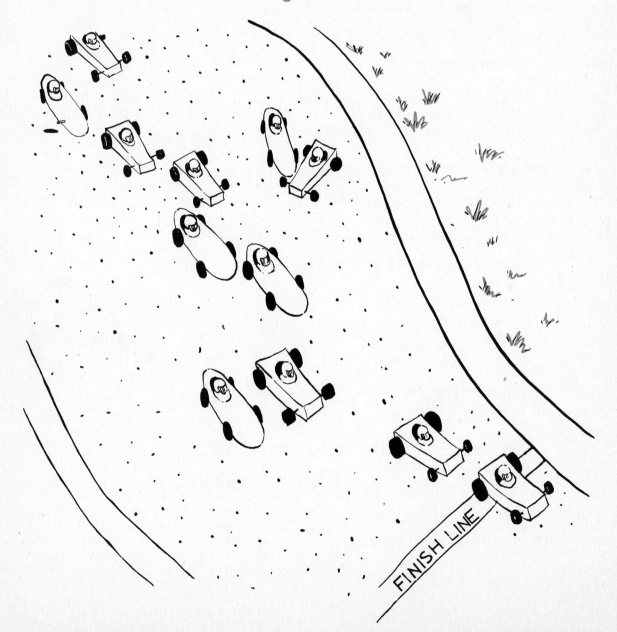

FINISH LINE

60

C When did it happen? <u>Underline</u> the right answer.

1. When did car number twelve finish the race?

    a. before car number eight

    b. after car number eight

    c. in a tie with number eight

2. When did car number six come in?

    a. It did not finish the race.

    b. It came in last.

    c. It came in fifth.

3. When did car number five come in?

    a. It tied for third place.

    b. before car number eight

    c. after car number twelve

D Write a sentence to answer each question. Start the sentence with a capital letter and end it with a period. The first one has been started for you.

1. What happened to cars four and three?

    Cars four and three

    _____

2. Why didn't car number six get started?

    _____

3. Which cars were in a tie for third place?

    _____

4. Which car came in fourth place?

    _____

5. Which car came in sixth place?

    _____

6. Why didn't car nine finish the race?

    _____

E Draw lines to match these.

1. a day of the week   twelve

2. stopped so that it won't work   October

3. finish at the same time   stuck

4. tenth month of the year   Saturday

5. It makes a car stop.   drive

6. make the car go   tie

7. in back of   beside

8. next to   wheel

9. something on a car   behind
   that rolls on the ground   brake

10. three more than nine   second

F Which word belongs in the sentence? Write the word.

1. Families build cars for the race in _____.
   (Often, October, Other)

2. Before the race, Chuck washed his car to get it _____.
   (class, clean, close)

3. We must _____ by so we will not wake the baby.
   (creep, cry, camp)

4. The people _____ the gun start the race.
   (hair, happy, heard)

5. Jenny came in _____ in her yellow car.
   (started, Sunday, second)

6. The people saw the race from the _____.
   (field, filled, fish)

7. Each race car had four _____.
   (wheels, weeks, whales)

8. There was a _____ for third place in the car race.
   (tiny, tie, toy)

9. The cars stop at the end of the race by using

their _____. (buttons, berries, brakes)

10. The car door was _____ and we could not open it. (stung, start, stuck)

G **Ms. Black writes for the newspaper. Read what she wrote about last week in Butterfield.**

On the first day, I went to a big fire on Winter Street. A house burned and a girl got three children out. On the second day, I went to a football game and the home team lost. I wrote a story about a bus crash on the third day. On the fourth day, I watched the Butterfield school children plant two trees in front of the school. A TV star came to Butterfield on the fifth day and I talked to him and took his picture. A truck full of fish turned over on Main Street on the sixth day.

Here are the dates when Ms. Black wrote stories. Put the right story name under the date when it happened.

1. **Monday, October 6**   4. **Thursday, October 9**

_____   _____

2. **Tuesday, October 7**   5. **Friday, October 10**

_____   _____

3. **Wednesday, October 8**   6. **Saturday, October 11**

_____   _____

Story Names

a. School Gets a New Look
b. House Burns on Winter Street
c. TV Star Comes to Town
d. 1,000 Fish Swim on Main Street
e. Butterfield Bees Lose 14 to 0
f. Bus Crashes

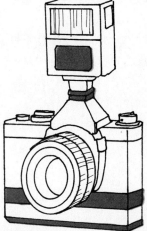

63

When Barby was born in October, Dad planted a dogwood tree. Every year Barby and the tree grew larger. When she was seven, Barby started to see that she and the dogwood tree kept changing together.

In May, Barby told Mom and Dad, "The dogwood tree has beautiful pink flowers on it now. I am different, too. I don't wear my winter coat anymore. I am wearing my light clothes."

Mom said, "Yes, the dogwood tree has flowers every spring. The days get warm and you change your clothes, too."

Barby kept watching the dogwood tree. By June, the tree had lost its pink flowers. It was wearing dark green leaves. Barby was not wearing a coat because the summer days were hot.

July, August, and part of September went by. One day Barby saw that the dogwood tree had red berries on it. The days were getting cooler and Barby was wearing her red jacket outdoors.

"Dogwood, we are eight years old today," Barby told the tree in October. The leaves and berries on the tree were redder. The fall days were colder and Barby wore her red coat outdoors.

All the leaves fell off the dogwood tree in November. Barby had to wear her hat, coat, scarf, and gloves to go outdoors. The days were cold through the winter months of December, January, and February.

"Isn't it strange?" said Barby to Mom and Dad. "The dogwood tree and I change with every season of the year. But in winter it wears nothing and I must wear many clothes to keep warm!"

A <u>Underline</u> the right answer.

1. What is this story about?

   a. Trees grow much faster than children.

   b. Barby has a birthday party every year.

   c. Every season people and trees change.

2. When did Dad plant the dogwood tree?

   a. when Barby was born

   b. when Barby was seven

   c. in the spring

3. Barby's birthday was in which month?

   a. September   b. October   c. May

4. The dogwood was planted at which time of year?

   a. spring   b. summer   c. fall

5. What is on a dogwood tree in the fall?

   a. flowers   b. berries   c. nothing

6. What is on a dogwood tree in the spring?

   a. flowers   b. berries   c. nothing

7. What were the days like in December, January, and February?

   a. very hot   b. very warm   c. very cold

8. What did Barby think was strange?

   a. The days were colder in the winter.

   b. The tree had nothing on it in the winter.

   c. Dad planted another dogwood tree.

9. What is the best name for this story?

   a. Barby and the Dogwood Change

   b. The Dogwood Leaves

   c. Barby's New Red Coat

B Draw lines to match these.

1. came into life

2. not inside the house

3. bigger

4. becoming different

5. a short coat

6. something to keep hands warm

7. something to keep the neck warm

8. one of four times of the year

changing

born

larger

outdoors

scarf

November

season

jacket

gloves

C What time of year is it? Write the name of the season over each picture.

| The Four Seasons |
| winter   spring   summer   fall |

1. _____

2. _____

3. _____

4. _____

D **Write the name of the season that each story tells about.**

The Four Seasons			
winter	spring	summer	fall

1. This season is very, very hot. People want to stay under the trees to keep cool. Windows in houses are left open. Everyone wants cold drinks and ice cream.

   _____

2. It is so cold outside, people must keep their houses warm inside. Some people burn wood. Schools must be kept warm, too. People wear coats, hats, and gloves outdoors. Dogs get thick fur to keep them warm.

   _____

3. Green leaves change into beautiful red, yellow, orange, and brown leaves. Then they fall to the ground. Nuts fall from trees, too. Squirrels save the nuts.

   _____

4. Tiny new green leaves start to come out on trees and plants. Beautiful flowers come out on some trees. Many bugs and animals are born.

   _____

5. The days are getting cooler. The days are not as long as they were. Leaves cover the ground. People rake the leaves. Children start back to school for another year.

   _____

6. Birds fly back from their winter homes. They build new nests and lay eggs. The rain turns the grass green. New flowers start to push up out of the ground. Days are getting warmer.

   _____

E Write the name of the month that comes next. Use the list of months.

Twelve Months of a Year			
January	February	March	April
May	June	July	August
September	October	November	December

1. September, _____, November

2. May, _____, _____, August

3. February, _____, April, _____

4. July, _____, September, _____

5. March, _____, _____, June

6. December, _____, _____

F When did these things happen? Look back at the story for help.

January	February	March	April
May	June	July	August
September	October	November	December

1. Put a black **X** on the three winter months when Barby must wear warm clothes.
2. Put a yellow star on the month when Barby was born.
3. Put a brown circle around the month when the dogwood tree had pink flowers.
4. Put red berries on the fall month when Barby saw that the dogwood tree had berries.
5. Put a blue box on the last month of the year.
6. Put a purple ✔ on the summer month when the dogwood tree lost its pink flowers.
7. Put a red circle around the month of your birthday.

G Mother started a baby book when Barby was born. Mother wanted to remember the dates when Barby started to learn new things. Here is part of the baby book. Read this story. Then write the right things next to each date.

Five months after Barby was born, she learned to sit up. The next month she learned how to drink from a cup.

Barby learned how to crawl when she was seven months old. At eight months, Barby could stand by herself.

Four months later, Barby was one year old. She learned to walk alone for the first time.

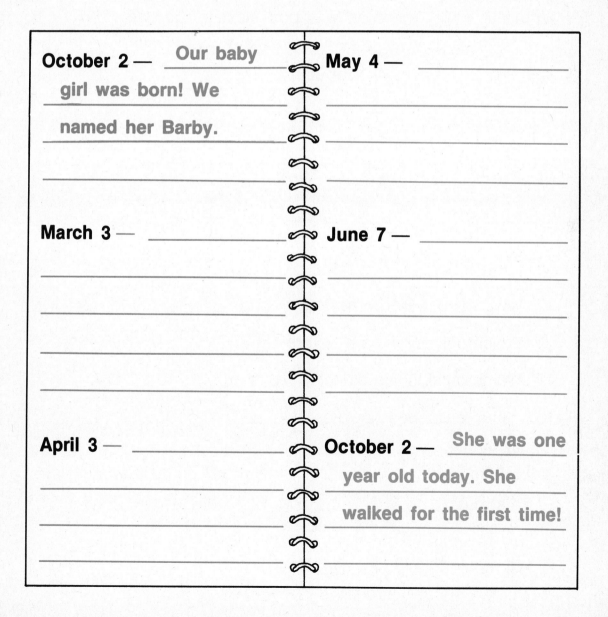

October 2 — _Our baby girl was born! We named her Barby._

March 3 — _____

April 3 — _____

May 4 — _____

June 7 — _____

October 2 — _She was one year old today. She walked for the first time!_

A These children are in the same class. They were all born the same year. The name of the month when the child was born is under each picture.

Danny	Sam	Ruth	Wen	Ella	Chang

February	June	March	January	May	April

Now, write the children's names in order, starting with the oldest. Write the month the child was born next to the name.

	Name		Month Born
1.	**Wen**	—	**January**
2.	_____	—	_____
3.	_____	—	_____
4.	_____	—	_____
5.	_____	—	_____
6.	_____	—	_____

7. Which two were born after Chang? _____ and _____

8. Which child was born before Danny? _____

9. Which child is the oldest? _____

10. Which child was born last? _____

B Which word fits the sentence? Write the word.

1. Cats must _____ milk with their tongues to drink.
   sick   lick   pick

2. We stood on the sidewalk to _____ the cars go by.
   whisker   which   watch

3. My tongue is in my _____.
   month   mouse   mouth

4. Never talk to _____ people on the street.
   change   orange   strange

5. Many red _____ fell off the tree this fall.
   berries   babies   brooms

6. We had to _____ to make you hear us.
   yellow   yell   yesterday

7. The children will have a _____ after school.
   middle   midnight   meeting

8. There are four _____ in one year.
   seasons   seconds   sidewalks

9. A dogwood tree is _____ our house.
   beside   between   because

C   **Which one comes next? Pick a word from the box to write.**

spring	fall	Tuesday	Thursday
January	July	grandfather	first
noon	night	fifth	

1. Monday, _____, Wednesday

2. _____, second, third, fourth

3. morning, _____, afternoon, evening

4. May, June, _____, August

5. winter, _____, summer, fall

6. eighth, seventh, sixth, _____

7. December, _____, February

8. _____, Friday, Saturday

D Read this story. Under it is Scott's book where he puts good pictures. Can you help fix the book? First, put the dates in the book. Then, find the pictures on the next page. Put the letter and name of each picture under the right date in the book. The first one is done for you.

On Thursday night, the second of September, Scott took a picture of a family of raccoons as they crept into a field to get a meal of sweet corn.

On September third, Scott saw a snake resting beside the tomato plants near the fence.

"That will make a good picture," said Scott. Snap!

The next morning Scott walked to Tenth Street. He saw a big truck stuck in the mud on a hill. Snap!

On Sunday, the fifth of September, Scott saw a little red flower coming up in a crack in the sidewalk. Snap!

The next afternoon Scott took a picture of two teams playing a football game. Snap!

On Tuesday he took a picture of a house that was built many years ago.

Scott's Picture Book

1. Thursday, September ____2____

   b. A Good Meal
   _____

   _____

2. Friday, September _____

   _____

   _____

3. Saturday, September _____

   _____

   _____

4. Sunday, September _____

   _____

   _____

5. Monday, September _____

   _____

   _____

6. Tuesday, September _____

   _____

   _____

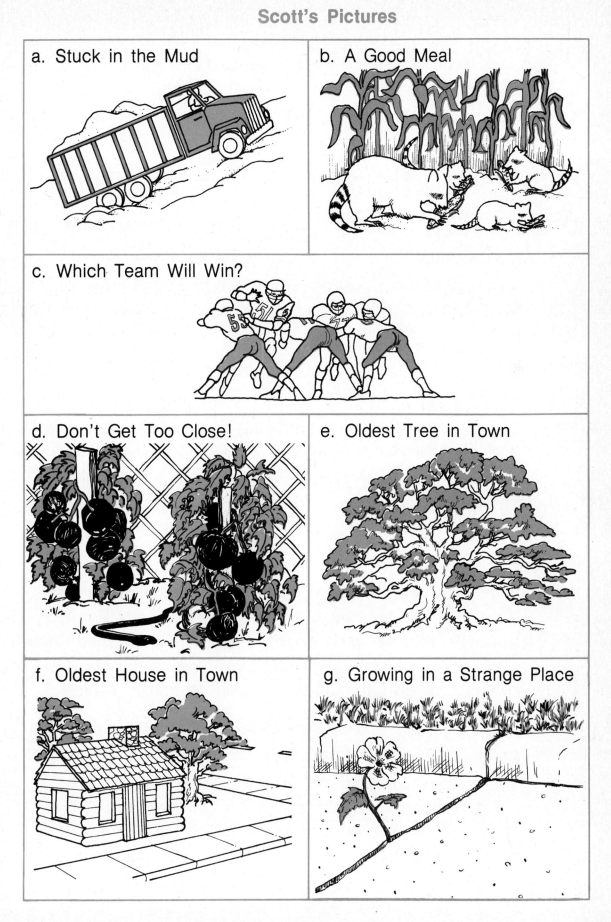

a. Stuck in the Mud

b. A Good Meal

c. Which Team Will Win?

d. Don't Get Too Close!

e. Oldest Tree in Town

f. Oldest House in Town

g. Growing in a Strange Place

Many children go away to camps in the summer. Here are some notes from campers to their mothers and fathers. Who wrote each one? Put the right camper's name under the note.

Campers		
Betty Bluewhale	Teddy Turtle	Jack Jones
Benny Bear	Sandy Skunk	Octy Octopus

1. Hello Mom and Dad,
   I love it here at camp. Today Mrs. Rockfish took us to an old boat on the bottom of the sea. We were looking for a treasure. I found it first because four of my arms kept everyone away. My fifth and sixth arms dug in the sand. My seventh and eighth arms picked up the treasure!

   Love, _____

2. Dear Mother and Father,
   You will be happy to hear how kind I am. Every day at lunch and dinner I give away my pie, cake, or ice cream. I eat my meat and lettuce. Uncle Brad said that I am kind to the others.

   Your kind child, _____

3. Dear Dad and Mom,
   I can take care of myself now. Today at camp we raced to a bees' hive full of honey. I got there first. Benny Bear pulled me away. He said he was bigger. I showed him. I turned my back and started to spray. I sprayed him between the eyes! He will smell for weeks. Now no one comes near this beehive!

   Love, _____

4. Mom and Dad,
   Please come to camp and take me home. I don't like it here at all! I am up in a tree by myself. No one will come near me. They say I smell bad. It happened when I got to the bees' nest before Sandy Skunk did. The skunk sprayed me!

   Your sad son, _____

F The words **up** and **down** are **opposites**. The words mean very different things. Write the opposite for each word in the list. Use the words in the box.

last	before	under	morning
hot	near	top	back
dry	tiny	the	lost

1. wet _____

2. found _____

3. evening _____

4. far _____

5. front _____

6. over _____

7. after _____

8. cold _____

9. first _____

10. bottom _____

G Read this story. Then write a paragraph that tells what you think happened next.

Mr. and Mrs. Bird built a beautiful nest near the top of a thin dogwood tree. They worked very hard.

In April, four little eggs were in the nest. Mrs. Bird sat on them morning, noon, and night. She had to keep them warm.

A hungry bear came by one Friday.

"I will eat Mrs. Bird and all the eggs," said the bear. He moved closer to the tree.

Mrs. Bird heard the bear and started to call for help. She felt afraid.

What happened to Mrs. Bird and the eggs?

_____

_____

_____

_____

_____

_____

① The children had been at the big park all morning and all afternoon with Mack's father. They had gone on many rides and had seen many funny things. The hot September sun had made them tired. Some children were resting. They were waiting for Mack's mother to pick them up at six o'clock.

② Kate said, "Look at that strange little animal."

③ They saw a tiny brown animal with black and white stripes down its back. It had a furry tail. Its tail was thinner than a squirrel's tail.

④ "That's a chipmunk," said Sandy, who was the oldest child. "Stay very still."

⑤ "Yes," whispered Joe. "Chipmunks are afraid of people. Don't let it know we are here."

⑥ The children watched the tiny animal run along the ground. Then it sat up on its back legs. It put its front paws up to its mouth. The chipmunk did this many times.

⑦ "I see something very strange," whispered Beth. "See how the chipmunk's face has changed!"

⑧ "Its cheeks are getting fatter and fatter!" said Ted.

⑨ The tiny animal's cheeks were all puffed up. Every time the chipmunk's paws went to its face, its cheeks got larger.

⑩ "I know why," said Ted. "It must have the mumps!"

⑪ "Poor, sick little chipmunk!" said Della.

⑫ "That is not why its cheeks are getting fatter!" said Sandy.

A **Underline the right answer.**

1. What is this story about?

   a. how an animal's cheeks looked larger

   b. the chipmunk's home

   c. rides the children went on at the park

2. Why do you think the chipmunk's cheeks looked larger?

   a. It had the mumps.

   b. It was holding food in its mouth.

   c. It was blowing up a balloon.

3. When was Mack's mother coming?

   a. at midnight   b. in the evening   c. at noon

4. How did the children feel after the day in the park?

   a. tired   b. smaller   c. furry

5. What do you think Mack's mother will do with the children?

   a. take them into the big park

   b. take them home

   c. help them catch the chipmunk

6. What did the children think was wrong with the chipmunk?

   a. It was hungry.

   b. It was not happy.

   c. It was sick.

7. What do we know about chipmunks?

   a. They have large noses.

   b. They have fur on them.

   c. They have feet like birds.

8. What is a good name for this story?

   a. Rides in the Park

   b. A Trip to the Zoo

   c. Watching the Chipmunk

B Detective Sharp Eye says, "You will need good eyes to know who is talking." Write the name next to the sentence.

1. Ann said, "A chipmunk has stripes." _____

2. "Della, what other tiny animal has stripes down its back?" asked Mack. _____

3. "That animal acts strange," whispered Mack. _____

4. "Stand still," said Joe, "because the chipmunk is afraid of us." _____

5. "Here comes the car now, Sandy," said Kate. _____

6. Now, look back at the story on page 76. Who is talking in paragraph ②? _____

7. Who is talking in paragraph ⑦? _____

8. Who is talking in paragraph ⑩? _____

9. Who is talking in paragraph ⑤? _____

10. Who is talking in paragraph ⑫? _____

11. Who is talking in paragraph ⑪? _____

C Draw lines to match these.

1. small animal with fur   strange

2. talked very softly   resting

3. sitting quietly   furry

4. not as fat as   chipmunk

5. part of the face   oldest

6. thin lines of color   whispered

7. in need of rest   thinner

8. the first one born   stripes

9. different; not like others   tired

                                             cheek

78

D These marks " " are clues. They tell you what someone said. This mark " is just before the first word someone said. This mark " comes just after the last word someone said. Put a (circle) around any mark that is not in the right place in the sentences. One is done for you.

1. Joe ⊗said, Chipmunks are afraid of people."
2. "Is the chipmunk here?" asked Mack's mother in the car.
3. "Yes," said Della. "Look at the " sick little animal.
4. "Oh!" It has the mumps, Ted," said Sandy.

E Someone is talking in some of these sentences. No one is talking in other sentences. Put these marks " " in the right places to show what is said. Then tell who is talking.

1. Tomorrow I'm going to Bob's birthday party, said Joe.

   _____

2. Mack said, I'm going too. Let's get Bob something for his

   birthday. _____

3. I'm on my way to the store now, said Joe. Come with me.

   _____

4. Mack and Joe went to the toy store. They saw many toys to

   buy. They did not know what to get. _____

5. Then Joe saw a puzzle. He said, This is what I want to get for

   Bob. _____

6. I'll get this ant farm, said Mack, because Bob likes bugs.

   _____

7. But his grandmother won't let Bob keep bugs in the house,

   said Joe. _____

8. Bob likes to build things, said Mack. I'll get this race car and

   he can put it together. _____

Read the cartoons. What are they talking about? Then answer the questions on the next page. Write complete sentences for your answers.

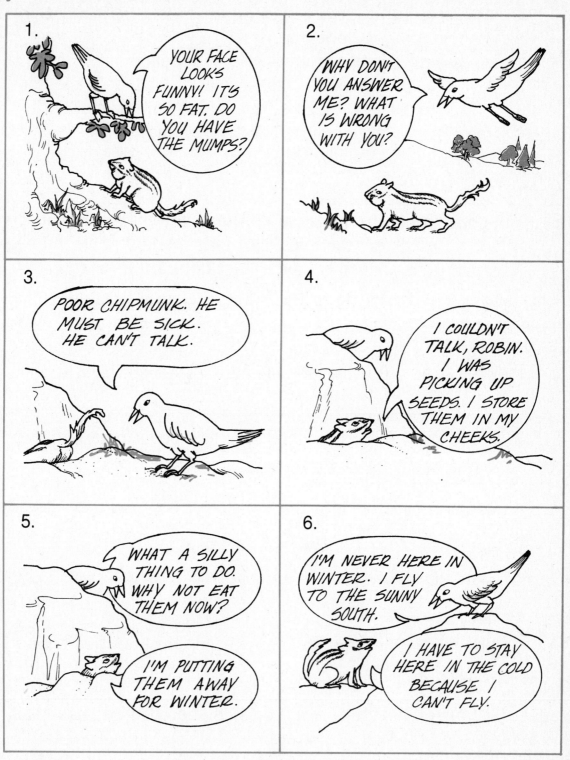

1. What made the chipmunk's cheeks so fat? _____

_____

2. Where did the chipmunk take the seeds? _____

_____

3. Why must the chipmunk store seeds? _____

_____

4. Why doesn't the robin store food for winter? _____

_____

5. Why didn't the chipmunk talk to the robin at first?

_____

6. What makes you think that this may not be a true story?

_____

_____

7. Where did the chipmunk carry the seeds? Underline the right answer.

   a. in its arms

   b. in its cheeks

   c. on its back

   d. in its chin

8. Where does the robin go for the winter? Underline the right answer.

   a. to sleep under the ground

   b. to a warm place

   c. into people's houses

   d. on an airplane

9. Why can't the chipmunk go south? Underline the right answer.

   a. It is too poor.

   b. It is too big.

   c. It gets lost.

   d. It has no wings.

When Leon played hide-and-seek with his friends, he always hid in places where no one would think of looking for him. Today he squeezed between two bushes near an open place under the back steps.

Ugh! He bumped into something sticky. It got all over his face, his hair, his hands. In the sticky goo were little dried dots of stuff.

What a surprise! It was a huge spider's web.

The other children never found Leon that day. He was back in his bedroom looking at the Table of Contents of a book. He was trying to find out what those ugly little dots of stuff were in the spider's web. He did not want something so awful on his face ever again.

Stories We Like

Table of Contents

PAGE

Part 1. Our Neighbors 5
    New Neighbors Next Door 6
    The House Across the Street 12
    The Man with Five Cats 17
    Jan's Grandmother Comes To Visit 22

Part 2. Funny Stories 27
    Teddy Spills the Milk 28
    The Day We Bumped into a Skunk 34
    Worm Pie 42
    The Umbrella with a Hole in It 50

Part 3. Strange Animals 60
    The Spider's Web 61
    The Otters' Mud Slide 68
    The Chipmunks' Home 75
    How the Tiger Got Its Stripes 86

A **Underline** the right answer.

1. How many parts are in this book?

   a. one   b. three   c. two

2. What is the first part of the book about?

   a. people who live near us

   b. strange animals

   c. people who live far away

3. Which part has stories that will make us laugh?

   a. Part 1   b. Part 2   c. Part 3

4. On which page is there a story about otters at play?

   a. page 17   b. page 42   c. page 68

5. In which story do you think somebody got wet?

   a. The Man with Five Cats

   b. The Umbrella with a Hole in It

   c. The House across the Street

6. Which story will be about an animal's fur?

   a. Worm Pie

   b. New Neighbors Next Door

   c. How the Tiger Got Its Stripes

7. Where in the book can we read about animals that are different?

   a. Part 3, page 60

   b. Part 2, page 27

   c. Part 1, page 5

8. What does the table of contents tell about each story?

   a. the page the story starts on

   b. the page the book ends on

   c. how many pictures are in the story

Detective Sharp Eye wants to know, "Can you tell which story each picture came from?" Use the story titles on page 82. Write the story title under the picture. One is done for you.

1. The Otters' Mud Slide

2. _____

3. _____

4. _____

5. _____

6. _____

C **Draw lines to match these.**

1. something to keep rain off us   visit

2. person who helps us learn   cover

3. the outside of a book   umbrella

4. to go to someone's house   teacher

5. little animal with brown fur   contents

6. list of stories inside a book   title

7. name of a story or book   neighbors

                                        otter

D **In which story might this be found? Look back at the story titles in the table of contents on page 82. Write the right titles and page numbers below.**

1. An old house is across the street from ours. It has no windows. The door is falling off. No one lives there.

    _____   _____

2. The skunk turned around and banged its feet. A bad smell came out and made our eyes hurt. We ran away!

    _____   _____

3. A teddy bear comes to life when the family is asleep. One night Teddy spills some milk. The family finds out about Teddy.

    _____   _____

4. That is where a spider lives. And that is how a spider gets food to eat. The spider catches bugs in it.

    _____   _____

5. The apple pie was ready to eat. We started to cut into it. Something long and thin was wiggling in the pie.

    _____   _____

6. Dad went to the airport to pick up his mother. She was coming to stay with the family for a week.

    _____   _____

E **Can you make a table of contents? Use these story titles. Put them in the right part of the book.**

Story Titles

a. Across the Sea in Sailboats
b. Schools in the Old Days
c. The Long Walks
d. Cutting Wood for the Fire
e. How Children Helped at Home
f. How Horses Helped People
g. Building a Fireplace
h. Children's Games
i. Keeping the Campfire Going
j. Wagon Making
k. Toys of the Old Days

Table of Contents	PAGE
1. How They Went from Place to Place in the Old Days	4
	5
	12
	22
	30
2. How They Kept Warm in the Old Days	36
	47
	54
	61
3. Children in the Old Days	68
	69
	80
	88
	95

F **Something is strange about these pictures. <u>Underline</u> the sentence that tells what is strange about each picture.**

1.

   a. The umbrella is in his hand.

   b. The umbrella is under his feet.

2.

   a. Tigers do not go to zoos to see the people.

   b. People do not go to zoos to see the tigers.

3.

   a. The chipmunk's nose is in the wrong place.

   b. The chipmunk's tail is in the wrong place.

4.

   a. Skunks do not have feet.

   b. Skunks do not wear shoes.

5.

   a. Worms cannot learn to read.

   b. Glasses help worms read faster.

6.

   a. People move into houses.

   b. Houses cannot move.

13

Ranger Smith said, "There has been little rain this year. The trees and grass are very dry."

"Yes, everyone must be more careful in the woods now," said Ranger Reed. "After you finish with your campfire, put it out."

"Put water on the fire," said Ranger Smith. "Stamp on it. Put sand on it. Push the wood around."

"Never leave a fire until all the sparks are put out," said Ranger Reed.

Then the rangers told us about two different families.

Ranger Smith said, "The Peach family was camping out in the woods in June. They slept each night in sleeping bags in their tents. On their last morning here, they cooked breakfast over a fire."

"Then they packed all their things. Mrs. Peach put water on their fire to put it out. Mr. Peach stamped on it. They waited until no fire was left. Then the Peach family got into their car."

A **Underline the right answer.**

1. What do you think the Peach family will do next?

   a. They will run the car over the fire.

   b. They will drive away.

   c. They will call the fire fighters.

2. Where do you think the Peach family will go next?

    a. home

    b. back into the tent

    c. to visit a neighbor

3. What did they cook over the fire on the last day?

    a. dinner   b. supper   c. breakfast

4. When did the Peach family go camping?

    a. July   b. June   c. January

5. Why do you think they used tents?

    a. to keep the fire burning

    b. to keep warm and dry

    c. to stop the fire from burning

    Then Ranger Reed said, "The Stone family was in the woods, too. They were not careful. They made a campfire. When they were ready to leave, they did not put water on the fire. They just left the fire burning. They got in their car and went on down the road."

6. What do you think could happen next?

    a. The family could get a new car.

    b. The fire could keep on burning.

    c. The rain could put the fire out fast.

7. Why is it a bad idea to leave a fire burning?

    a. The food will not be good.

    b. The woods may catch on fire.

    c. The next campers won't want your fire.

8. What is a good title for this story?

    a. How To Put Out Fires

    b. How To Build a Fire

    c. How To Be a Ranger

B Pick the word from the box that means the same thing. Write the words on the lines.

burning	camping	careful
finish	ranger	slept
sparks	stamp	tent

1. someone whose job is taking care of the woods— _____

2. on fire— _____

3. to hit your feet down on something— _____

4. sleeping and eating in the woods— _____

5. come to the end— _____

6. small bits of fire— _____

7. a place to sleep outdoors— _____

8. trying to be safe— _____

C The town of Butterfield was having its Fourth of July picnic. Many people were there when a fire started. Very quickly, fire was all around the picnic grounds.

Five roads went out of the picnic grounds. Four roads were not safe, because the fire had reached them. Only one safe way was left.

The fire fighters told people to go out this way. People who listened were safe. Can you get out by doing what the fire fighters said to do? Draw a line on the map on page 91 to show the safe way out of the picnic grounds.

1. First, take the road that goes under the bridge.
2. Next, go past the outdoor cooking grills.
3. Then go by the big flower garden.
4. Then go past the swimming pool to the playground.
5. Go through the playground to the ball field.
6. Go by the ball field.

7. Now you must go across the brook to a big white house.
   The fire cannot reach here. You are safe!

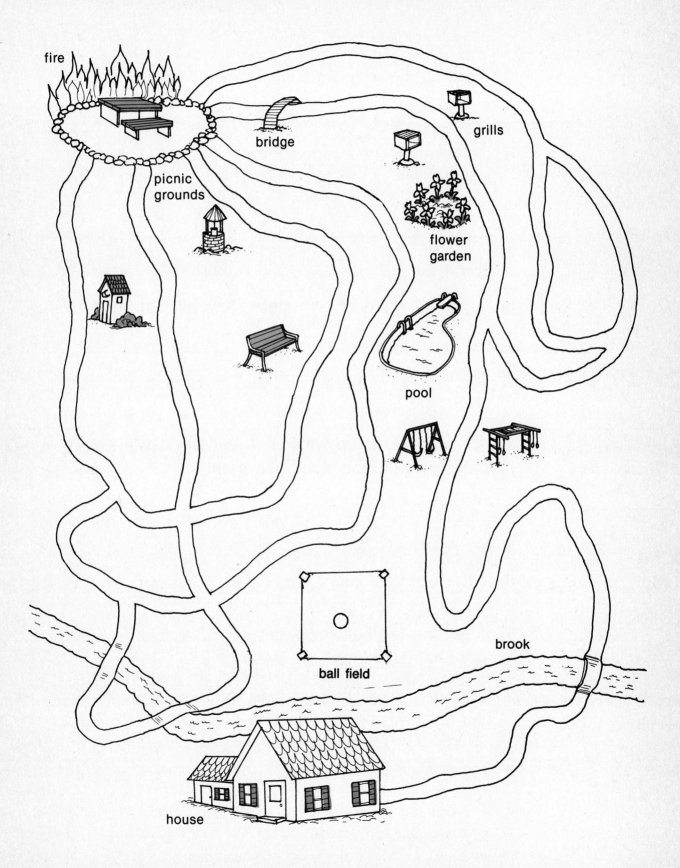

fire

bridge

grills

picnic
grounds

flower
garden

pool

ball field

brook

house

D Are you careful to do things the safe way? Read each pair of sentences. Put **S** by the safe way. Put **NS** by the way that is not safe.

_____ 1. If the light is red, hurry across the street on your bike.

_____ 2. If the light is red, wait for a green light before you go across on your bike.

_____ 3. Don't run in the halls at school. You may fall or run into someone.

_____ 4. Run in the halls and you will get to your room faster.

_____ 5. Never put toys on steps. Someone may fall on them.

_____ 6. Put toys on the bottom step. They will not be in anyone's way.

_____ 7. The best way to learn to swim is to jump into deep water. The water will hold you up.

_____ 8. Don't go into deep water if you cannot swim. Have someone with you when you swim.

_____ 9. When you ride in a car, don't put your arm too far out the window.

_____10. Never put your arms out of car or bus windows.

_____11. When the fire bell rings, get in line as fast as you can. But clean your desk off first.

_____12. When the fire bell rings, walk into line as fast as you can. Look at the teacher and do what you are told.

_____13. If a bee comes near you, hit it fast with a book.

_____14. If a bee comes near you, stand still. Don't move fast. The bee will go away.

E Detective Sharp Eye says, "Look at the pictures. What do you think will happen next? Circle the right sentence."

1.
   a. A car may hit her.
   b. She will win the race.
   c. A dog will run after the car.

2.
   a. The animals will help put out the fire.
   b. The animals will run away.
   c. The animals will drive off in their cars.

3.
   a. He will fall and get hurt.
   b. He will get clean this way.
   c. He will get on a bus.

4.
   a. She will call the fire fighters.
   b. She will change the tire.
   c. She will get a new car.

5.
   a. The clothes will get burned.
   b. He will put on the clothes.
   c. The clothes will get clean.

6.
   a. Someone will take a bath.
   b. The clothes will be washed.
   c. The floor will soon be wet.

It was not warm outdoors. All the trees were brown and gray, because they had no leaves on them. The children moved fast on the ice. What fun they had!

A **After you read each part of the story, <u>underline</u> the right answer to each question.**

1. What time of year do you think it is?

   a. summer   b. spring   c. winter

2. What month might it be?

   a. May   b. August   c. January

3. What do you think the children are doing?

   a. swimming   b. ice skating   c. dancing

4. What do we know about the ice?

   a. It is hard and cold.

   b. It is soft and wet.

   c. It is warm and soft.

5. Why do you think the trees have no leaves?

   a. It is summer.

   b. It is too cold for leaves to grow.

   c. Bugs ate all the leaves.

Nearby, a steep hill was covered with deep snow. There was some light from the moon. Children rode down the hill and shouted to each other. Then they walked back up the hill, singing and laughing.

6. What time of day do you think it was?

   a. noon   b. night   c. morning

7. What do you think the children were riding?

   a. bikes   b. horses   c. sleds

8. How do you think the children feel?

    a. hurt   b. happy   c. hungry

9. What do you think it is like outdoors?

    a. cold   b. warm   c. hot

10. Why are the children walking back up the hill?

    a. The horses can't go up the steep hill.

    b. They can sing better when they walk.

    c. Sleds cannot ride up the hill.

    All the children on the snowy hill had on heavy clothes and boots. Some children wore gloves and others wore mittens. They wore heavy caps and earmuffs to keep their ears warm. A heavy scarf was around each child's neck. All the children's noses were red and shiny.

11. What did the children have on?

    a. warm clothes   b. sun hats   c. umbrellas

12. Jack's sled was going down the steep hill. When did the sled get to the middle of the hill?

    a. before it got to the bottom

    b. before it got to the top

    c. after it got to the bottom

13. Why were the children's noses red and shiny?

    a. They had used red paint.

    b. They had been eating red berries.

    c. It was very cold outdoors.

14. Where did they wear gloves and mittens?

    a. on their ears

    b. on their feet

    c. on their hands

1. Which of these do you think Sam will say? Write it in the right place in the cartoon.

   a. "Nice jump, cat!"

   b. "Bad cat! We can't eat pie today!"

   c. "Bad cat! I'll have to show you how to jump better."

2. Draw lines to match the answers to the questions.

   a. Why did the cat jump?

   b. What will Sam have to do next?

   c. Who was at the door?

   eat the pie
   throw the pie away
   Grandmother
   eat the cat
   to get down to the floor

More fun! Read another cartoon.

1. Which of these do you think Mother will say? Write it in the right place in the cartoon.
   a. "A whale sprayed water on our house."
   b. "The sky fell on us."
   c. "There is a big hole here."

2. Draw lines to match the answers to the questions.

   a. Why did the water come in?

   b. When will water come into the house again?

   c. What must the people do now?

   the next time it rains

   when the sun shines

   fix the hole

   A hole was in the floor.

   A hole was in the roof.

D Draw lines to match these.

1. moving on ice   heavy

2. something we ride on snow   mittens

3. how a high hill may be   shouted

4. thick   sled

5. yelled   skating

6. gloves without places   steep
   for each finger
                                                              winter

E Detective Sharp Eye says, "What can you learn from these stories? <u>Underline</u> the answer to each question."

The farmer had many chickens in the hen house. One hen was sitting on her nest. Six eggs were in the nest. Soon four baby chicks came out of four of the eggs.

1. What do we know about the farmer's chickens now?

   a. He does not have as many chickens now.

   b. He has more chickens now.

   c. He has the same number of chickens now.

2. How many eggs did not hatch?

   a. two   b. six   c. five

Five children were drinking milk. Fran put a lot of ice in her milk. The other children did not want ice.

3. What do we know about Fran?

   a. She likes hot milk.

   b. She likes warm milk.

   c. She likes very cold milk.

4. How many children did not want ice in their milk?

   a. three   b. four   c. two

98

Two children were going to the store to buy paint sets. Lee had eight dollars. Lisa had six dollars. The paint sets were $7.85 each.

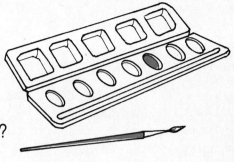

5. What do we know about the girls?

   a. Lisa got a paint set.

   b. Lee got a paint set.

   c. Lisa and Lee got paint sets.

6. What do we know about the money?

   a. Both girls must get more money.

   b. Lee must get more money.

   c. Lisa must get more money.

7. What will happen after Lee buys the paint set?

   a. She will get change from her eight dollars.

   b. She will not get any change back.

   c. She will give the store nine dollars.

8. Who had less money?

   a. Lisa   b. Lee   c. Less

The days were getting colder. Tim went to get his old jacket. He tried to put it on. He could not wear it because it did not fit him now.

Dad said, "We will have to buy you a new jacket for the fall." Dad took Tim to the store. Now Tim has a new jacket that fits him.

9. What do we know about Tim's old jacket?

   a. It was too large for Tim.

   b. It fit Tim.

   c. It was too small for Tim.

10. What time of year did Tim need a new jacket?

   a. spring   b. fall   c. summer

Donna and her friends had a club. The children met every Thursday to read detective stories. The detective club was saving money to buy a new video detective game.

One Thursday afternoon, the club met at Ellen's house. The children put their money together on top of a table.

All at once Ralph said, "Look at your baby brother, Ellen!"

The baby was painting the walls and a chair with Ellen's paints.

"Stop, Bert!" shouted Ellen. "Bert has just learned how to climb out of bed by himself. Now he gets into everything!" Ellen picked Bert up.

Liz said, "I'll hold him."

"I'll put all the money away," said Donna, "so Bert can't grab it!"

Ellen gave Donna a big red wooden box for the money. Just then Bert pulled away from Liz. He bumped into the fishbowl. Water, bits of glass, and fish fell all over the floor. Then Bert grabbed the money from the table.

Donna took the money away from Bert. Then she ran into the kitchen with the box and the money. She opened the big box. Inside was a smaller box. Donna opened it. Inside that one was a very small box. Donna put the money in it.

As she was putting the boxes back together, the middle one fell. The lid got a crack in it. Donna hid the boxes in the kitchen.

Ralph was settling Bert in his bed for a nap. Ellen was cleaning off the paint. Mark was sweeping up glass. Liz was putting the goldfish into a glass of water.

"Where is the money now?" asked Ellen.

Donna went into the kitchen to open the boxes. The money was gone.

"Who took the money?" Donna asked her friends. "It was right inside here!" She showed them the big box.

Ralph said, "Was it? Maybe you put it in the middle box, the one with the crack in the lid."

"Be like Detective Sharp Eye, Donna," said Liz.

"Let's see if you can find out who took it!" said Mark.

Then Donna knew. Her detective friends were playing a joke. They were trying to find out how good a detective she was.

Donna thought. At last, she said, "It can't be Ellen. She has paint on her hands. There is no paint on the box."

Donna said, "Mark cleaned up the wet bits of glass. Liz picked up the wet goldfish. But this box is dry. So we know they did not put their wet hands on the box."

"That leaves you, Ralph," said Donna. "Give me the money, please."

"I didn't take it," whispered Ralph. "Little Bert did."

"No, he didn't!" yelled Donna. "I knew you did it as soon as you said the middle box had a crack in it. I had just dropped it. No one but the person who took the money and I knew about the crack. I kept that middle box hidden in the big box to trap you!"

"Well, Donna, you've learned a lot from Detective Sharp Eye!" said all the children.

Underline the right answer.

1. What is a good name for this story?

   a. The Pretty Boxes

   b. Donna, a Good Detective

   c. Bert Learns To Paint

2. Why did someone take the money?

   a. to buy a paint set

   b. to buy more goldfish

   c. to see if Donna could think like a detective

3. When was the money taken?

   a. when the children were cleaning up

   b. before Bert made a mess

   c. when Donna was in the kitchen

4. How did Donna know who took the money?

   a. Liz told Donna who took the money.

   b. The child told about the crack in the middle box.

   c. Bert saw the child hide the money.

5. What was the story mostly about?

   a. a video game

   b. a baby who got into everything

   c. someone who could think like a detective

6. How did Donna know who had *not* taken the money?

   a. The boxes had paint on them.

   b. The boxes were wet.

   c. The boxes were clean and dry.

7. What was Ralph doing when Donna hid the money?

   a. putting goldfish in a glass

   b. sweeping glass bits

   c. putting the baby in his bed

B A dictionary tells what words mean. The words in a dictionary are in ABC order. This is called alphabetical order. Look at the picture dictionary. Answer the questions.

Animals

donkey A donkey helps people work.

hippopotamus A hippopotamus eats water plants.

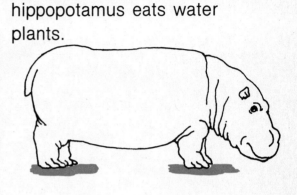

eagle An eagle is a large and strong animal.

kangaroo A kangaroo hops.

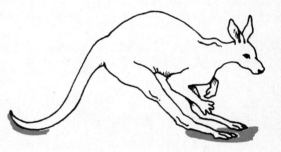

1. Which animal has feathers? Write the word. _____

2. If the word **lizard** were on this page, where would it be found? Underline the right answer.

   a. before **donkey**

   b. between **hippopotamus** and **kangaroo**

   c. after **kangaroo**

3. If the word **camel** were on this page, where would it be found? Underline the right answer.

   a. before **donkey**

   b. after **eagle**

   c. between **donkey** and **eagle**

Read the cartoons. What are they talking about? Then answer the questions on the next page. Write good sentences for your answers.

1. What were Ralph and Ellen doing? _____

_____

2. How long had the children worked on the puzzle? _____

_____

3. Why did Ellen and Ralph go out of the room? _____

_____

4. What will Mom do? _____

_____

5. What do you think Baby Bert is saying in the last picture? Write
what you think he said. Put it in the cartoon too.

_____

_____

D Write the word that goes in each sentence. Use the words
below.

club	video	sweeps	save
cleaned	cracked	shouted	

1. He _____ the
   floor to clean it.

2. The kitchen needs
   to be _____.

3. The _____ meets
   every Friday.

4. A _____ game can
   be played on a TV
   screen.

5. Why don't you _____
   your money until
   you need it?

6. When the egg fell on
   the floor, it
   _____.

Use this table of contents to answer the questions below.

Table of Contents

PAGE

Part 1. Nests on the Farm 3
      Ducks' Nests 7
      Chickens' Nests 11
      Turkeys' Nests 14

Part 2. Nests on Rocks 17
      Nests near Water 21
      Nests up in the Hills 26
      Nests in Cold Lands 30

Part 3. Nests in Trees 35
      Birds' Nests 39
      Insects' Nests 41

Part 4. Nests on the Ground 45
      Birds' Nests 48
      Insects' Nests 54

1. What is the book all about? _____

2. Name four places where nests are found.

   _____   _____   _____   _____

3. Write the page numbers where you can find out about these.

   _____ a. a robin's nest in a tree

   _____ b. where a turkey builds a nest

   _____ c. nests near water

   _____ d. two places where insects build nests

   _____ e. where a chicken lays eggs

   _____ f. where duck eggs can be found

4. What kinds of nests are in this book? Circle the answer.

   a. nests of snakes   b. nests of frogs and tadpoles

   c. nests of birds and insects   d. nests of fish

B **These pictures belong in the book about nests. Use the table of contents on page 106 to tell in which part of the book you would find each picture. Write Part 1, or Part 2, or Part 3, or Part 4.**

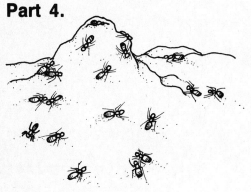

1. _____

2. _____

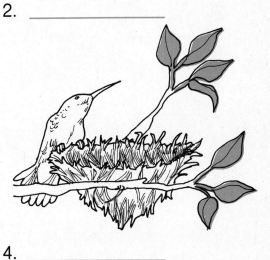

3. _____

4. _____

5. _____

6. _____

C (Circle) the right word to end the sentence.

1. If it is a skunk, it has (sparks, stripes, spots).

2. If a flower has colored dots, it has (sparks, stripes, spots).

3. If the otter is warm, it has (for, fire, fur).

4. If logs are burning, we see (for, fire, fur).

5. If snow is clean, it is (white, with, wheel).

6. If you are careful, you will be (soft, sail, safe).

D Put a word from the puzzle into each sentence.

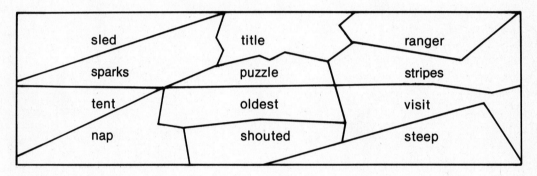

sled   title   ranger
sparks   puzzle   stripes
tent   oldest   visit
nap   shouted   steep

1. We can't find three of the _____ parts.

2. Some _____ from the fire burned the flowers.

3. The baby takes a _____ every morning.

4. What is the _____ of the book you like best?

5. The tiger has black _____ .

6. Grandmother is the _____ one in our family.

7. Let's take a _____ to sleep in when we go camping.

8. I want to be a _____ and work in the woods.

9. My aunt is coming to _____ us for a week.

10. The teacher said we _____ when we should have whispered.

E **What do you think will happen next? <u>Underline</u> the best answer.**

1.

   a. He will fix the tire.
   b. He will buy a new bike.
   c. He will paint the tires.

2.

   a. She will get a broom to fix it.
   b. She will get a needle and thread to fix it.
   c. She will ask a mother hen to fix it.

3.

   a. He will put out a fire.
   b. He will see some sparks.
   c. He will clean the floor.

4.

   a. Flowers will grow in them.
   b. They will walk away.
   c. They will get dry.

5.

   a. The pen will get too heavy.
   b. The balloon will get too heavy.
   c. The air will come out of the balloon.

6.

   a. The ball will fly away.
   b. The ball will go up in the air and come back down.
   c. The ball will change into a balloon.

F Write **yes** or **no** after each sentence.

1. If there is a heavy rain, the ground will get wet. _____

2. If people are flying, they must be on an airplane. _____

3. If grass is growing, it is getting taller. _____

4. If you jump into a swimming pool, you will get dry. _____

5. A ranger is too heavy for you to carry. _____

6. If you want your little brother to go away, put a stamp on him

   and drop him in a mailbox. _____

7. If you are careful, you can build a safe fire. _____

8. Mittens keep people's feet warm. _____

G What can you learn from these stories? <u>Underline</u> the answers.

   Four children wanted to play a game. But the game box
said that six people were needed to play the game.

1. What do we know about playing this game?

   a. The children must get more people to play.

   b. The children do not need more people to play.

   c. They have too many children to play the game.

2. How many children do they still need to get?

   a. four   b. three   c. two   d. no children

   Dad was cooking eggs for breakfast. He cooked one
egg for each of the family. There were five in the family.
Dad has twelve eggs in the house.

3. What do we know about the eggs?

   a. Dad had eggs left after breakfast.

   b. Dad needed more eggs for breakfast.

   c. There were no eggs for breakfast.

4. How many eggs were left after breakfast?
   a. eight   b. seven   c. three   d. no eggs

H Put these marks " " in the right places to show what was said. Then tell who is talking. If no one is talking write no one. One is done for you.

Ralph   Donna   Liz   Detective Sharp Eye

1. "Hello, Detective Sharp Eye!" said Ralph. _____Ralph_____

2. Good afternoon, Ralph, said Detective Sharp Eye.

   _____

3. The children played a game with the detective.

   _____

4. Liz whispered, You are a good detective, Donna.

   _____

5. The detective said, Good detectives must think.

   _____

6. What is wrong in this story, Liz? asked Donna.

   _____

7. She said, Jack looked out of his window at midnight. In the bright sunlight, he saw the robbers behind the barn.

   _____

8. Liz and Ralph thought for a long time. _____

9. Ralph did not answer. _____

10. Jack could not see the robbers in the sunlight. The sun is not out at midnight, said Liz. _____

11. Good thinking, Liz, said Donna. _____

1 **Where is Detective Sharp Eye? Use the letters next to the pictures. Put the right letter by each story.**

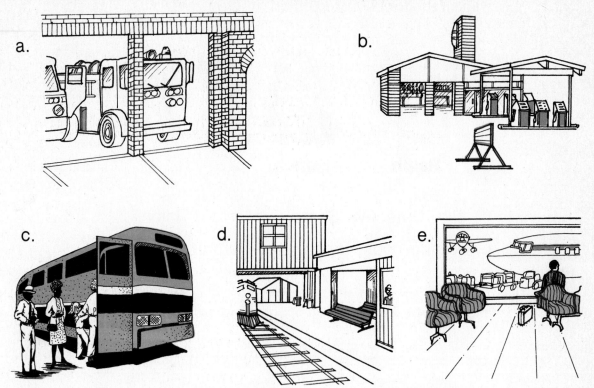

_____ 1. Detective Sharp Eye is very tired. He just pulled off the road to get something fixed on his car. He is resting and waiting for the car to be ready. Then he will drive on.

_____ 2. Detective Sharp Eye is in another place. He must hurry to another city to work. He has a ticket and he is waiting. Soon something will pull up. It will make a lot of noise as it rides on the tracks. It will quickly carry Detective Sharp Eye far away.

_____ 3. Now Mr. Sharp Eye is in a different place. He is getting in line with other people to buy a ticket. They are all going to another town. They will be riding together and resting as the driver takes them along the road. The driver will check the tires before they leave.

_____ 4. Now Detective Sharp Eye is in a small town. He is in a big place with trucks all around him. Each truck is red and some have ladders. Many people work in this place. They put out fires.